Suits & Pajamas
A Memoir of Grace, Grit and Becoming

T'JUANA ALBERT

Publisher: Rise2Write Publishing LLC

PAPERBACK ISBN: 979-8-9950800-1-5

HARDCOVER ISBN: 979-8-9950800-2-2

Library of Congress Control Number: 2026907282

www.rise2write.com

This is a work of non-fiction. This memoir is based on the author's personal experiences and recollections. Some names, identifying details, and circumstances have been changed to protect the privacy of individuals. Certain events and dialogue have been reconstructed from memory. The author's reflections and interpretations are presented in good faith.

For information about custom editions, special sales, premium and bulk purchases, please contact: authortjuanaalbert@gmail.com

THIS BOOK WAS NOT WRITTEN OR EDITED USING ANY FORM OF AI.

DEDICATION

To the Next Generation

For the ones coming after me—
may the road be wider,
and the weight lighter.

"Children have never been very good at listening to their elders, but they have never failed to imitate them."

—James Baldwin

Table of Contents

Note from the Author

This book is not a blueprint.

It is not a how-to guide, a leadership manual, or a prescription for healing. What you're holding is a record of one life lived in motion. One that is shaped by responsibility, survival, faith, and the quiet work of becoming.

I didn't write this because I have everything figured out. I wrote it because I have lived long enough to recognize the difference between endurance and wholeness, between performance and truth. For many years, I believed success required carrying everything without complaint. I believed composure was protection. I believed rest had to be earned. I know now that those beliefs kept me functioning, but not always free.

These pages trace the moments that shaped me: childhood instability, loss, adoption, motherhood, corporate leadership, caregiving, love, and faith. Some stories are tender. Others are unfinished. All of them are honest. I share them not to be admired, but to be useful and to offer language for experiences many of us carry quietly. I hope to remind you that freedom is not an arrival, but a choice we make again and again.

If you see yourself here, know that you are not alone. If you recognize your own patterns, be gentle with yourself. And if this book gives you permission to set something down, then it has done its job.

PREFACE

When I look back at the world my parents inherited, I'm struck by how much weight they were already carrying before they ever held me in their arms. In the early 1950s, for Black families in America, especially in the rural South and Southwest, life had a way of blending beauty and struggle so tightly that you couldn't always tell where one ended and the other began. Sundays were survival set to music; choirs lifting us higher than the world ever intended.

Evenings belonged to the blues; voices pouring from cracked speakers, singing our pain back to us without apology. Communities leaned on one another because the country refused to truly see us, no matter how loudly it claimed progress. Its residue lingered everywhere; in neighborhoods, in opportunities, and in the limits the outside world tried to place on our lives.

Still, inside Black homes and gathering places, there existed an entire universe of laughter, resilience, and pride. It wasn't loud pride, or something worn for applause. It was quiet, steady, and quietly defiant. The kind that let you believe in possibility even when the world insisted you had no right to it. Even now, when I think of that world, I can almost smell the cigarette smoke trapped in winter coats, hear church shoes on wooden floors, feel the way adults talked around pain like it could hear them.

West Texas shaped that possibility in its own fierce way. The land stretched out flat and wide, the kind of horizon that made you feel like the world went on forever. But for Black folks, that same horizon rarely opened into opportunity. Towns were scattered like far-off islands, and survival demanded more than just hard work. It required determination, grit, and a kind of faith that didn't always come easy. People worked long shifts in cotton fields, oil fields, kitchens, and factories, then came home to raise children, put food on the table, and keep hope alive with nothing more than a prayer and a cracked vinyl record.

Radios crackled with gospel Sunday mornings and blues on the weekends, each song a reminder that joy and suffering often lived in the same house. Neighbors kept watch over one another's children as though they were their own. Aunties—some blood, many not—acted like the world's first responders, quick with a pot of beans or a sharp word meant to set you straight. Church ladies seemed to know when someone needed a hot plate, a few dollars, or simply to be seen and pastors making house calls. The land itself could feel unforgiving, but the people made it livable. Community was the well everyone drew from.

 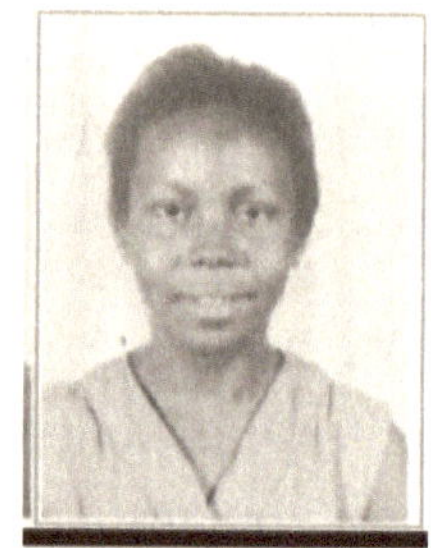

Imagining my parents inside that world, at nineteen (dad) and seventeen (mom), nearly kids themselves, brings the truth into painfully sharp focus. They weren't standing at the threshold of adulthood; they were shoved into it. My mother was seventeen, still a girl navigating the unresolved trauma of her own upbringing. My father was nineteen, barely steady on his own two feet. When they discovered they were pregnant with me, the world around them didn't ask if they were ready. It told them they had no choice. They were forced into marriage before either of them understood what marriage required. They hadn't healed from their pasts, hadn't built dreams for their futures, and suddenly they were supposed to build a family.

The pressure must have felt suffocating, no diplomas, no savings, no roadmap and very little room for mistakes. They faced racism from employers, judgment from family members, and expectations that far exceeded their maturity. They were responsible for a life before they had figured out how to care for themselves.

And yet, they tried. They did what the people around them had always done. They pushed forward with whatever strength they had. That strength, however, came with cracks. Deep ones.

My mother carried the burden of responsibility in ways her young heart was never prepared for. She was the one who stayed home, the one who raised the two children, and the one who shouldered the resentment she never had the tools to name. I know now that part of her resented me before I even arrived. She resented that my existence forced her into adulthood long before she was ready. That resentment shaped the way she mothered me. It shaped the silences, the sharp words, the distance that stretched between us even when we were in the same room.

My father, on the other hand, believed providing meant paying the bills and little more. And in that one narrow sense, he was reliable. But in every other way a father is supposed to show up—in presence, in protection, in nurturing—he fell short. He ran the streets, chasing distractions or maybe just chasing the version of himself he hoped existed somewhere. I don't think he understood that his absence carved gaps into my younger brother Wil and me. Gaps that would take us years to confront and even more years to heal.

Growing up, Wil and I became the collateral damage of two people trying to navigate adulthood with childlike tools. The lessons we learned didn't come from wisdom or guidance; they came from chaos, instability, and survival. Our parents were doing the best they could, but "the best they could" still hurt. It shaped us, molded us, and forced us into a kind of resilience we didn't ask for.

This prologue is to lay the foundation, not blame. It's about truth. It's about naming the world I was born into, so readers can understand the world I eventually built for myself. Because nothing about my early life pointed toward the life I have now—an executive career, a dream home, a loving husband, daughters I adore, and grandchildren who light up my world. None of that was handed to me. None of it came easily.

I grew up in the aftermath of my parents' youth, their trauma, their forced decisions, and their limitations. But I also grew up with a front-row seat to the kind of resilience that runs deep in Black families, especially in places where hope isn't a guarantee but a choice. My story is not about the extraordinary childhood I had; it's about the extraordinary life I built despite the childhood I didn't.

Before I ever learned how to drive on the freeway, I learned how to survive the shoulder.

This is a memoir about trauma, yes. But more than that, it is a memoir about hope. The kind of hope that rises from broken places, from imperfect parents, from cultural landscapes shaped by hardship, and from the deep well of strength that I didn't know I possessed until I needed it.

This is where everything begins.

PART I

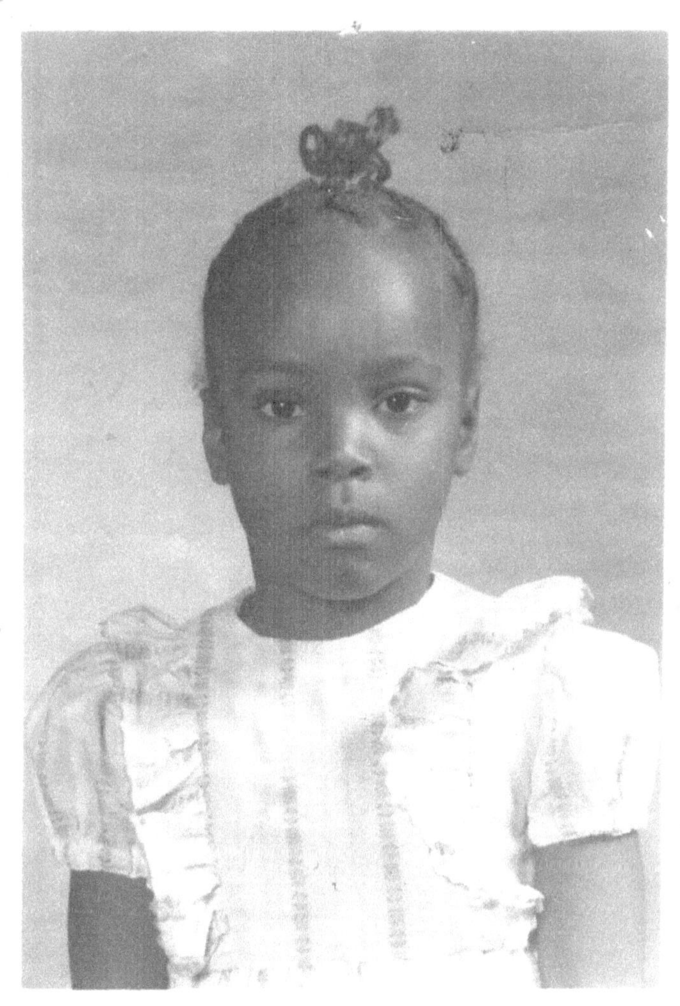

Chapter 1: THE FIRST TIME I DISAPPEARED

S harp. Exposed. Impossible to shake.

I was five years old, standing on the playground of my first elementary school in Dumas, Texas, and I knew without anyone telling me that I didn't belong. Not in a quiet way. Not in a way you could ignore.

I felt different in the kind of way that makes your stomach twist and your face burn. It wasn't the kind of difference that earns attention. It was the kind that invites harm.

The wind in Dumas was always doing the most. It whipped across flat land with nothing to slow it down, carrying dust and the faint smell of livestock. The playground sat out in the open like something forgotten. No trees. No shade. Just metal swings too hot to sit on and a slide that burned the back of your legs by noon. Kids ran through that space with the wild freedom children have when they've never had to think about whether they belong.

I had.

I was the only Black kid in the entire school, or at least it felt that way. If there were others, they were tucked into corners I never reached. The yard stretched wide, a sea of blond and brownish-blond heads glinting in the sun. Their laughter rippled across the playground, light and easy.

Mine stayed trapped somewhere inside my chest.

I don't remember what sparked it. I'm not sure if someone bumped into me, stared too long, or simply decided they needed someone to aim their cruelty at that day. But suddenly a small group of boys closed in around me, and everything in their faces told me I was the chosen one.

They called me the N-word with rehearsal-level precision. Like it was part of a game they played often. They spit it out with the kind of boldness only children who have heard that word spoken freely at home can muster.

I didn't know what it meant.

I didn't understand why their eyes shifted when they looked at me, or why their mouths twisted into something sharp and satisfied.

But I knew what it felt like.

Shame teaches its language long before you learn the dictionary definition.

I stood there, frozen. Not fighting back. Not running. Just staying still, the way children of my era were taught to do. Children were trained to be seen and not heard, even in pain. Even in fear. You kept quiet. You kept still. And whatever happened at home, at school, anywhere in between, especially the bad things, you never told.

No adult stepped in.

No teacher shouted.

No friend pulled me away.

It was just me in the middle of that wide Texas heat, surrounded by words I didn't yet understand but would spend a lifetime learning.

I did the only thing I knew how to do.

I stood there and took it.

I wouldn't realize until decades later how deeply that moment planted itself inside me. How it trained my body. How it shaped my instincts. I learned the art of enduring silently, the reflex to shrink instead of fight, the belief that mistreatment was something to survive rather than confront.

Trauma rarely announces itself. It slips in quietly and takes up residence before you know how to lock the door.

But something else was present too, even then, though I didn't have language for it yet. A softness beneath the sting. A presence in the absence. The quiet voice I would later come to know as God. I didn't know how to call on Him yet, but somehow, He was already there.

When the bell finally rang, it felt like air rushing back into my lungs.

I grabbed my little backpack, clenched the small house key hanging from a chain around my neck, and sprinted to the taxi waiting out front. My mother always tucked taxi money under her favorite china dish in the cabinet, just enough to get me home safely while she and my dad were working.

Before the divorce, we lived well. My father worked hard at the meat packing plant, and it showed. We had the kind of home people nodded at approvingly. Nice clothes. Plenty of food. Toys for Christmas and birthdays. Everything a child could need, at least on paper.

But the house felt void of affection. It lacked warmth. I have no memories or feelings of being held by my parents. Surely, they must have. But if they did, there is no imprint in my heart.

So when the taxi turned onto our street, what washed over me wasn't joy or anticipation.

It was relief.

The relief of a child who knows that silence, at the very least, won't call you names.

I unlocked the front door and stepped into a house where no adult would be home for hours. My mother always left a honey bun warming in the oven, wrapped in foil so it stayed soft. It was care in its most practical form, even if it wasn't the tenderness I needed.

Wil, only three then, was usually at childcare. So the house was still. No voices. No footsteps. No questions. No comfort, but no danger either.

I sat at the kitchen table with my backpack still on and nibbled that honey bun slowly for a long time. The sweetness felt like the only kindness the day had offered.

I didn't cry.

I didn't speak.

I didn't have the vocabulary for what had happened.

Only the impact.

And somewhere between that playground and that quiet kitchen, I made an unconscious decision that would shadow me for years.

Get them to like you.

Whatever it takes.

Blend in.

Become agreeable.

Don't stand out for being Black.

Don't draw attention.

Stay small enough to stay safe.

I was five years old, and already learning the art of disappearing.

What I didn't realize then, what I couldn't realize, was that God had already begun His work in me. Even when I felt unseen, He never looked away. Even when I felt alone, He sat quietly beside me.

That peace I would later feel walking into church began here, in the silence of a kitchen lit by late-afternoon sun.

Part II

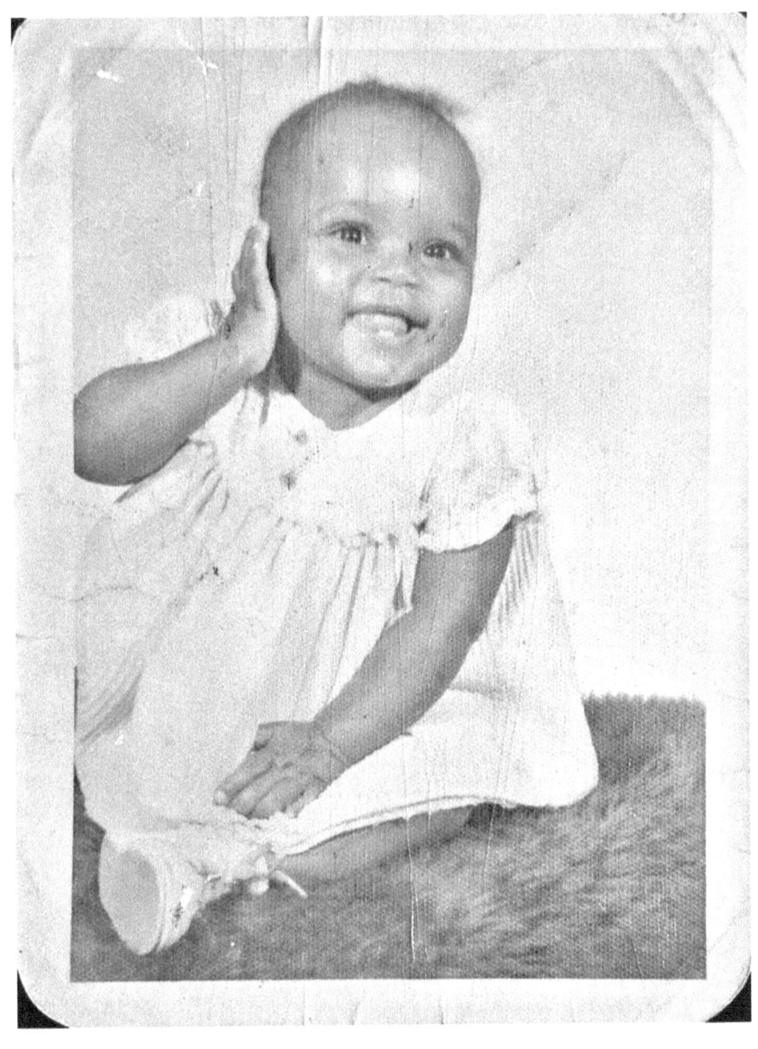

If childhood had a rhythm, mine was an offbeat, dynamic shifting tempo the moment I found my footing.

My parents were barely more than children when they began raising us. Three kids in three and a half years, all born in a small town called Hereford, Texas. I was born in 1970. Wil was born in 1972. And my baby brother, Warren LaShawn, though I only knew him as Shawn, was born in 1973.

Their marriage was built on expectation and obligation, not readiness. My mother had just turned seventeen when she became pregnant with me, still in school. My father was graduating from high school, primed for an athletic scholarship that could have changed the course of his life.

In our community, especially in that era, pregnancy didn't spark conversation.

It shut it down.

Pregnancy meant marriage. Full stop. And dreams adjusted accordingly.

They went from teenagers with possibilities to parents with responsibilities almost overnight. And what they couldn't name, they acted out. What they couldn't manage, they avoided. What they hadn't healed, they passed along.

But before the unraveling, before the disappearances and the disappointments, there were five of us, a young family moving through life the best way we knew how.

And then came October 1973.

Shawn died suddenly.

The circumstances were never clear. Was it SIDS? We will never know. What I do know is that his death left a loss so sharp it split open the already fragile seams holding my parents together.

Adults said he was "gone," but that word was too clean.

He wasn't gone. He was absent.

His passing created a heaviness in the air and a silence that echoed louder than the noise it replaced. It saddens me deeply that I have no real memories of him. But the aftermath etched itself in our family permanently.

My parents' grief was both quiet and volcanic. Quiet in the way no one ever seemed to speak his name. Volcanic in the way everything around us shifted and became unpredictable, smoky, and hot.

His death took more than him.

But it also took the version of my parents who might've existed had grief not swallowed them whole.

It changed the weight of everything, including my responsibility to Wil. He became more than my little brother. He became my purpose. My constant. My one non-negotiable.

And one night, in 1976, God proved why.

Wil and I shared a small bedroom. The kind where the beds were so close you could hear the other person breathe. Even in the dark, I could always sense Wil. I knew his tiny shifts and sighs, the cadence of his breathing.

But that night, something in the air felt wrong.

His breathing, normally soft and steady, came out in short, ragged gasps.

I called his name. Nothing.

I shook him gently. His body strained for air. Fear didn't even have time to rise. Children raised in instability don't hesitate. They act.

I dragged him, his small body heavy with struggle, across the floor and into our parents' room. My tiny voice sounded the alarm that night.

Everything after that blurred. My mother jolting awake. My father grabbing keys. The front door slamming. Headlights slicing the night as we raced to the hospital.

Collapsed lung.

Two words no child should ever need to understand.

And yet I did, as well as any six-year-old could.

Wil survived. But something in me shifted permanently. My instincts rewired themselves around him. Tight, immediate, unwavering.

I had a role.

I had to protect him.

I had to be the one to look after him because something deep in my spirit told me to hold onto him. The ground was going to shift.

And it did.

Life didn't get easier. It got louder. Messier. More transient.

From 1977 to 1986, we moved constantly. Once my parents separated, we moved from Dumas to Clovis, New Mexico. Then from Clovis to Chula Vista, California. Chula Vista back to Clovis. From Clovis back to Dumas. Then from Dumas to Spring Valley, California. Spring Valley back to Clovis. And finally, from Clovis to Phoenix, Arizona.

In all that shuffling, I attended eleven schools.

Eleven new beginnings.

Eleven silent negotiations with myself about how to survive the next cafeteria, the next classroom, the next set of kids scanning for weakness.

Survival, instability, and reinvention became the curriculum of my childhood.

Family anchored us, though not always in the ways people assume. Until about the age of seven, my father's presence was unpredictable. He floated in and out, unreliable in the everyday moments that mattered. But his family wrapped warmth around us. Aunts. Uncles. Cousins. Siblings. People who loved loudly even when life was hard.

Pre-divorce, Texas weekends meant cousins piled into living rooms, racing barefoot in the street, sipping water from outdoor sprinklers when we were thirsty because you were not allowed to run in and out of the house.

On my father's side, I remember aunties who hugged you tight and held on long enough for you to feel it. Aunt Eva Belle gave the best hugs because they always felt safe, like a hug from God Himself. She was the first memory I have of knowing what God felt like.

In those living rooms, crowded and loud, I felt something that soothed me.

Belonging.

Warmth.

A soft echo of the peace I would later find in church.

My mother's side was quieter then. Present, but not dominant. Until everything fell apart for her. After the divorce, the weight of being a single parent began to set in, and her life slowly started spinning out. This is when she started withdrawing, emotionally first, and sometimes physically.

It was her family, especially my grandparents, who stepped in. Different kinds of love. Different kinds of saving.

And then there was school.

It tested me every single day.

When we moved back to Clovis after my parents separated, the schools were more diverse. More kids who looked like me. More kids who didn't stare through me. But I learned quickly that diversity didn't guarantee acceptance.

In Clovis, I learned that even among "my own," hierarchies existed. Bullying became a weekly rite of passage. Diversity came with stratification.

There was a sliding scale of worth.

Who was pretty.

Who was popular.

Who was "too dark."

Certain things were said to me that took years to recover from. And it cut deeper because it came from Black people, my community.

"You're cute for a dark girl."

"Don't wear bright colors, they make you look darker."

Those words sliced quietly, cleanly. No playground needed.

I had already learned what it meant to be targeted for being Black.

Soon, I would learn what it meant to be targeted for being poor.

My mother's strain showed in the small things. Shoes with holes. Clothes that didn't fit right. Children notice everything, and they exploit it. They were relentless, and I was always somehow the easy target.

So, I sharpened the tools I had.

My mind.

My body.

My determination.

Straight A's became proof that I deserved to exist.

And track became the one place my body didn't betray me.

Running felt like freedom, like I could outrun shame, outrun hunger for approval, and outrun the need to shrink. It felt like God's breath at my back. It was the only space where my body wasn't something to be teased or diminished.

It was power. Speed. Purpose.

I didn't yet know these wounds would follow me into dating, into corporate rooms, into motherhood, into caregiving. I didn't know any of that yet. Back then, I was just surviving, learning new hallways, new faces, new rules.

Eleven times over.

The irony is that today, in corporate America, I adapt to change as easily as breathing. People are surprised by how easily I navigate chaos. Reorgs. Layoffs. Crises. I don't get rattled.

As if anything in corporate America could rattle a woman whose childhood trained her to pivot before she learned to spell the word.

Those skills weren't a conscious thought back then. They were curated out of necessity. Built for survival.

The fighting would come later.

Much later.

But Chapter One isn't about the woman I became. It's about the girl who kept trying to find peace in a world that shifted beneath her feet. A world she didn't seem to fit in.

Chapter Two is where the mirror appears. Where I begin to understand that the world had opinions about my beauty, my worth, and my place.

Opinions I would spend years unlearning and disproving.

The wound that taught me beauty had conditions.

Visibility had rules.

Worth had shades.

The wound that made me believe, for far too long, that I needed permission to take up space.

CHAPTER TWO: ELEVEN SCHOOLS

Long before I understood the language of race or beauty, America had already taught me its rules.

Beauty, as it was presented then, was light; effortless, uncomplicated, and unquestioned. It was smooth, straight, or gently curled hair that moved when you turned your head. It was skin that reflected the sun just enough, but not too much. It was femininity that felt gentle, palatable, and safe. These images were everywhere—on magazine covers at the grocery store, in television commercials, in sitcoms and variety shows that played in the background of our lives.

They weren't framed as ideals. They were framed as normal.

Everything else was measured against them and I was on the wrong side of every comparison.

By the time we moved to Clovis in 1977, just one stop in a string of relocations, I already knew that being different came with penalties. Dumas had taught me that. But at the tender age of seven, Clovis introduced something quieter and more confusing because this time the judgments didn't always come from white kids on playgrounds. Sometimes they came from people who looked like me.

Inside the Black community, beauty had its own hierarchy; one shaped by survival as much as preference. Light skin carried ease and a certain auto-acceptance of being better or more beautiful than the "darker" kind. Hair that fell or swung was admired. Hair that coiled tightly toward the scalp was "fixed" with perms; chemically disciplined, scrutinized, and discussed as a problem to be solved. Beauty wasn't denied outright; it was rationed, distributed carefully between the chosen and the overlooked.

I didn't yet understand that these beliefs were inherited, passed down from a country that had rewarded proximity to whiteness for generations and sadly still does. You need look no further than the 2024 US elections. But, I digress.

What I know now is that my place in that hierarchy was decided early, and it was unmistakable. I was dark. Not ambiguous. Just dark. Not someone paused over in admiration. And my hair—my hair made everything louder. Thick. Kinky. Determined to be exactly what it was. It didn't swing or fall or cooperate. It announced me before I ever spoke.

The teasing was relentless.

Kids called my hair "nappy" as if it were a flaw that needed fixing. They mocked its "stiffness," comparing it to a Brillo pad as if my head were something meant for scrubbing. For good measure, they would laugh when I tried to pull it back. I couldn't make a ponytail. The best I could muster was pigtails. They laughed when I tried to tame it, laughed harder when it sprang back. The comments followed me from classroom to playground to hallway, until they settled deeply into my bones.

At home, I tried to solve the problem the way little girls often do—by pretending my way into a different reality.

I used to wrap a bath towel around my head and let it fall down the sides of my face and back, imagining it was my hair. Long. Straight. Silky. The kind of hair that meant beauty without debate. I would stand in front of the mirror holding it in place, tilting my head just right, trying to catch a glimpse of a version of myself that made me feel less ugly.

I didn't like my hair then. It felt like a liability. Something that made me vulnerable. Something kids used against me. Something I wished I could trade in.

When my mother decided to perm my hair herself, it felt like hope. Like, maybe this would finally fix what everyone else seemed to see as wrong, and this would finally quiet the comments. But instead, the chemicals burned my scalp, and my hair was fried. Whatever fragile sense of worth I was trying to protect was gone.

There was no careful transition. No gentle repair. No easing into a new look. Nope. My hair was cut all the way down. Short. Close. Making me look like a boy.

And the teasing intensified.

Too dark.

Too nappy.

Now too masculine.

In a culture that already policed Black beauty tightly, I had fallen outside every acceptable line. Having the hurt come from my own community and sometimes family members dismantled whatever confidence I had managed to build. The Black kids who had learned the same hierarchy were desperate to prove they didn't belong at the bottom of it, so they pushed me down to make sure they rose.

I had no friends. I wasn't pretty enough. Not popular enough. Not chosen. There was no one pulling me aside to counteract the damage. No one there reminding me that my skin was beautiful, that my hair carried history, or that my skinny, lanky body was not a mistake. Silence filled that space instead, and into that silence the world poured its definitions deep inside of me.

Looking back, I see what I couldn't then: this cruelty had roots. It was adaptation. Survival. Beauty had become a kind of armor, and those who wore it well were handled more gently by the world.

Television reflected this back to me daily. It became one of the few places I searched for proof that someone like me could exist and still be admired. But even there, the options were limited. Black women on TV in the 1970s and early 1980s were rare, and when they appeared, most fit a narrow mold. Jane Kennedy. Polished. Light. Glamorous. Marilyn McCoo. Elegant. Soft. Effortless. They were beautiful, undeniably so, but they didn't look like me.

The women who came closest were often allowed space only if they were extraordinary or defiant enough to demand it. I remember watching *Get Christie Love!* and feeling something ignite inside me. Teresa Graves was bold. Commanding. Unapologetic. Like Pam Grier, she took up space without asking permission. She was our chocolate version of *Police Woman*, played by Angie Dickinson, bold in a world that wasn't built to expect her. And while I was a fan of *Police Woman*, I was riveted by *Get Christie Love!* In her, I caught a glimpse of the woman I could become, and that was very compelling.

Then there's the legendary, indelible Cicely Tyson.

Cicely Tyson did not fit the mold of what society deemed beautiful. She was uncompromising in being her authentic self. Yet, there she was on the biggest screen, embracing her darkness with a quiet strength and resolve to prove she belonged. I first saw her in the never to be forgotten Alex Haley's *Roots* and then in *Bustin' Loose* with Richard Pryor. She was this incredible woman who looked like me, and I, like her. For the first time, I saw myself reflected with dignity.

I was captivated.

But like Teresa Graves, she was the exception. Not the rule.

Most of the time, I watched television searching for myself and coming up empty. And when you can't find yourself reflected anywhere, you start to assume the absence means something is wrong with you or that there is no room for *your kind*.

At school, the comments continued. Sometimes blunt. Sometimes disguised as subtle advice or statements of fact.

"You'd be prettier if you were lighter."

"You're cute… for a dark girl."

"Your hair would look better if it was straight."

I sucked my thumb far longer than I should have, resulting in crooked, bucked teeth. Unsurprisingly, the kids got a kick out of that too. I was called "scatter matter mouth" and other hurtful things. I felt like Charlie Brown. I couldn't catch a break.

Each remark reinforced the same message: beauty had conditions, and I wasn't meeting them.

As I got older, I sensed how this pressure showed up everywhere, not just among kids, but among adults, too. I saw it in the choices Black women made to survive in a world that rewarded a specific kind of beauty. I never judged those who lightened their skin or altered their features. It always saddened me, but I understood the why behind it. I understood the pain that drives a person to negotiate their appearance just to move through the world with less resistance.

And if I'm honest, had I been wealthy enough, protected enough, desperate enough back then, I might have done the same.

That truth doesn't shame me. It reminds me how powerful the lie was.

Around the same time, poverty began making itself known in quieter ways. Shoes wore out quickly. Clothes didn't quite fit. Haircuts were practical, not expressive. And the kids noticed everything.

So, I adapted.

If I couldn't be the prettiest, I would be the smartest. If I couldn't be admired for how I looked, I would be respected for what I could do. Straight A's became my proof of worth. Something no one could take from me.

Running followed not long after.

I was eight years old when I first found my way to a track, tagging along with my older cousin at the AAU Junior Olympics. I hadn't come prepared. I hadn't come to compete. But once I was there, something in me woke up. The sound of feet hitting the track. The tension at the starting line. And I knew speed. I had always known I was fast. I mean, heck, I had beaten every boy in the neighborhood and all of the boys in my family. I knew these girls would be no problem.

I asked my cousin if I could sign up. Right there. On the spot. She said yes. I didn't have the right clothes or shoes. So, I took my shoes off.

In my light pink pants and white top, I lined up with kids who looked like they belonged there, kids with proper gear, parents watching from the sidelines, confidence rooted in support.

I felt exposed in every sense of the word. But when the race started, everything else disappeared.

Barefoot, I ran. And I won. Not once, not twice, but 5 times! Every race I ran or field event I participated in, I won!

After each race, people gathered around me. They clapped. They smiled. They asked my name. It was intoxicating in a way approval often is. That day, I learned something without language: winning brought approval. Performance brought safety.

Track gave me something no mirror ever had. When I ran, my body wasn't wrong. It was powerful. Nobody cared about my skin tone or my hair texture. They cared about the clock and who crossed the finish line first. That first barefoot race taught me something I would carry for years: that achievement could create a kind of safety. A fragile, conditional safety, but safety all the same.

By seventh grade, I ran varsity track with high schoolers, often in the coveted anchor position, the one trusted to bring it home. Coach Tanner and Coach Scroggins believed in me without reservation. To them, I was something extraordinary. But not extraordinary enough for anyone to come watch.

Not my mother.

Not my father.

Not a single family member. It was just me and the track.

It is a strange ache, performing miracles without witnesses. Break a record, win a race, and board a bus alone. Looking back, I now understand what I didn't then. I wasn't just running races. I was sending flares into the sky.

I wasn't just running.

I was pleading.

See me.

Choose me.

Love me.

Through it all, God stayed near. Quiet. Steady. Present. I felt Him most in quiet spaces, in church, in moments when comparison softened its grip. Peace found me before confidence ever did.

Today, I am no longer that little girl holding a towel to her head, hoping to pass for something else. But I honor her. She was navigating a world that told her beauty had prerequisites and worth had qualifiers. She did what she needed to do to survive.

It would take years to unravel that lie. Years to learn how to see myself through a different lens, one not driven by achievement, but by truth. I learned to loosen my grip on perfection and replace it with authenticity. Over time, the relentless push to *become* gave way to a deeper calling: to create space for others to rise. In time, I realized that the peace I felt walking into church as a little girl had been telling me the truth all along: I was never meant to prove my value. I was meant to reflect on it and help others remember theirs.

But that comes later.

For now, this is the chapter where the wound deepened and where the long work of reclaiming myself quietly began.

CHAPTER THREE: SANCTUARY

In the Black community I grew up in, poverty didn't announce itself.

No one stood around naming what we didn't have. No one used language that reduced our lives to scarcity. What defined us wasn't lack; it was connection. Family. Showing up. Love that filled the spaces where money didn't reach. If there was struggle, it stayed in the background. It was never allowed to become the whole story.

That's what made my grandparents' house feel like a sanctuary.

When my parents separated, and my mother moved us from Dumas to Clovis, we landed near her village, my grandparents, and her younger siblings. Because my mom was the eldest, her brothers and sisters weren't much older than me. Over time, it felt less like I had aunts and uncles and more like I had older siblings. That closeness would shape me in ways I wouldn't understand until much later.

My grandmother, who we called "Mama" for the longest time, cooked as if love itself lived in her hands. Greens simmered low and slow with ham hocks. Oxtails cooked until they surrendered. Fried chicken, red beans, cornbread. Her biscuits were made from scratch, layered and warm, filling the house with a smell that wrapped around you before you reached the table.

And the desserts—always from scratch. Peach cobbler bubbling at the edges. Pecan pies rich and dense. Banana pudding layered with care. Nothing fancy. Nothing wasted. Everything intentional.

Holidays were their own production. Turkey, ham, chitterlings, dressing—not stuffing—greens, yams, mac and cheese, boiled potatoes. Ten or twelve cakes. Just as many pies. Everyone got to make dessert requests, and Mama never disappointed. Peach cobbler and sweet potato pie were always my favorites.

What amazed me most was how she did all of this in a tiny kitchen— twelve by twelve at most—with a four-burner stove and a single oven. And yet the food was always piping hot when it hit the table.

Neighbors and extended family drifted in and out, welcomed without question. Somehow, twenty people fit into a thousand-square-foot house with one bathroom, and no one ever complained.

You could walk into her home carrying the weight of the world and leave full in ways that had nothing to do with food.

My grandfather, our beloved Pops, showed love differently, but just as clearly. He worked a blue-collar job at a tire station and brought his paycheck straight home. Every time. He kept twenty-five dollars for gas and handed the rest to my grandmother to manage. No speeches. No posturing. Just responsibility. She packed his lunch and made sure he had three full meals every day.

Faith lived there too, even when no one made a point of naming it. Going to church with my grandparents was never dramatic; it was simply part of the rhythm of life. Sunday mornings, familiar hymns, scripture read with reverence, prayers spoken plainly and with urgency. God wasn't introduced to me as an answer to hardship or a solution to problems. He was introduced as presence. Steady. Watching. Available. Long before my life taught me how much could be taken away, faith taught me that something could remain.

They never talked about struggle. They didn't need to. Their love showed up in action. In consistency. In care. That model sank into me long before I had words for it.

Outside their home, life felt far less certain.

Up until around the age of nine, I felt fairly close to my mother, not deeply bonded, but tethered. Then came the night that shifted everything.

She asked me to go with her to the laundromat late, around eleven o'clock. I didn't question it. I rarely did. We sat under harsh fluorescent lights, the hum of machines filling the space as we folded clothes together. I remember watching her face, noticing a lightness I hadn't seen before. She looked happy. Anticipatory. Like someone standing at the edge of something new. She was downright giddy and chatting with me like I was her closest friend.

She was packing for a two-week trip with her boyfriend.

The next day, she dropped my brother and me off at my grandparents' house and left. Halfway through that trip, she decided she wasn't coming back. We didn't see her for months. When she eventually returned, it was only because the relationship had ended.

But something fundamental had shifted.

That laundromat night marked the moment I understood—without anyone explaining it—that my mother's joy didn't always include us. That she was searching for something beyond motherhood. That there was a crack in our stability, forming, and it was not something my brother or I could count on from her for very long.

While she was gone, it was my grandparents, my uncles, and one of my aunts who took care of us. Some of that care was nurturing. Some of it was complicated. But my uncles became anchors. Protectors. Consistent figures in a childhood that offered very little consistency. They showed up in ways my father hadn't, and our bond deepened through presence rather than promises.

It was no wonder that not long after, my mother met and married a man my brother and I barely knew.

He was in the Air Force, stationed at Cannon Air Force Base. His family was from Chicago. And though I never knew why, everyone called him "Jap". Things moved quickly, so quickly that one day he was just someone my mother talked about, and the next he was standing beside her as her husband.

I remember their wedding vividly. My mother wore a lime-green dress, her hair half up, curls bouncing as she moved. They married in the backyard of a friend's house just off Prince Street in Clovis. Their song was *"Groove With You"* by the Isley Brothers. Even now, that song carries me back to that day, to the rare sight of my mother looking genuinely happy.

Not long after, he legally adopted my brother and me.

At nine years old, I didn't understand the weight of that decision. I only knew our last names had changed overnight, without discussion, and it felt like it was supposed to mean permanence. I wanted to believe that.

For a little while, life felt steady, almost safe. Six months was about how long it took for things to permanently change.

Our adopted dad received orders that took him out of the country. I don't remember where he went. What I remember is the absence he left behind and how quickly everything unraveled. Soon after he left, my mother had a new boyfriend who moved in. And just like that, the man who had become our legal father disappeared from our lives.

We never saw him again.

But his name stayed behind, outlasting the man who gave it. Two fathers, both gone in different ways, and yet the name endured. Wil still carries it. His children carry it. Lindsay carries it. I carried it until I married. And though I had no real connection to the man behind it, giving up the name was harder than I anticipated. It had been one of the few things that kept me linked to my brother and my daughter.

As a child, I didn't have the language for what that meant. I only knew that everything about my life kept shifting—homes, schools, adults, even names—while I was expected to remain steady inside it all. Somewhere along the way, I learned that belonging was fragile and permanence something you hoped for quietly, without expecting it to last.

After her divorce from Jap, my mother was fully in the throes of single parenthood. She struggled. Her boyfriend at the time was abusive. We moved from a nice home to an apartment. No backyard. No friends coming over. Another new school. Our plates weren't as full. My clothes became worn and ill-fitting. The rubber sole of my shoe flapped so badly that I tied it together with a string.

I was in fourth grade, and the bullying intensified. I never started fights, but I became an easy target. The irony was that I won every fight I was forced into. Once, a bully held my brother "hostage" and told me I'd only get him back if I fought. I didn't hesitate. I beat him badly enough that he never bothered us again.

That was always true: if you came for my brother, I would destroy you. I didn't play when it came to him. Still.

Eventually, wanting a better life, my mother moved to California to live with her sister, leaving Wil and me with our grandparents again. We stayed in the same school, a small mercy. My grandmother made sure we were clean, clothes pressed, bodies lotioned head to toe. School clothes were preserved. Play clothes were separate. Pride mattered.

That summer, my mother sent for us again. Another move. Another school. Another apartment. Instability repeating itself. Food was scarce. We had oatmeal and toast for breakfast and dinner more times than I can count. Later, Wil joked we were so poor we couldn't afford Captain Crunch—only Lieutenant Crunch. We laughed about it years later. At the time, it hurt.

Sixth grade ended with us back in Clovis once more. Seventh grade passed in a blur of adjustment. Then eighth grade brought another shift: my mother left again, this time for Silver City, and Wil and I moved back to Dumas to live with our father.

That arrangement lasted one semester.

My father had remarried and was raising his new wife's young daughter. I felt immediately that I was tolerated more than wanted. Still, something important happened during that time.

I started playing basketball.

My favorite cousin Sheila was pretty, popular, and she had a boyfriend. She was everything I wanted to be. Since she played basketball, I wanted to follow her lead. I idolized her, and I wanted nothing more than to be just like her. Sheila was that girl everyone noticed. Basketball gave me another place to belong, another way to move my body, another outlet when words failed me. I was just finding my rhythm.

Like many things in my childhood, that semester ended abruptly. My father's wife and I got in a physical altercation that resulted in me running, literally from my dad's home to the safety of my uncle. And just like that, the next day, we were gone.

Basketball stayed with me. Track remained my first love, but basketball became part of my armor.

By the time I returned to Clovis, I was used to using my athleticism to quiet the storm around me. I was used to loss. Used to rebuilding. I had mastered the art of surviving instability by adapting quickly and expecting little.

I didn't know it yet, but those lessons about effort, endurance, and carrying weight quietly were shaping the person I was becoming.

And they were about to harden into expectation.

CHAPTER FOUR: COMPOSURE UNDER SURVELLANCE

R esponsibility didn't arrive in my life as a choice. It arrived quietly, as something decided about me rather than by me. It arrived the way expectations often do in families where stability is fragile, and hope needs somewhere to land. I didn't ask for it, and I didn't volunteer. I simply became the one everyone assumed would be fine.

I was the eldest. The firstborn. In families shaped by instability, firstborns don't just arrive first—they arrive assigned. Assigned meaning. Assigned expectation. Assigned responsibility for what comes next. Somewhere in the background of every adult conversation lived the unspoken hope that at least one of them would make it. And in the Black community, especially if you're a daughter, that "making it" comes with an extra layer: you're often expected to become the caregiver, the steady one, the one who circles back for everybody else.

At first, no one said any of this out loud. When I was younger, I was quiet, observant, and careful not to take up too much space. No one predicted anything extraordinary for me. That narrative didn't form until my grades became impossible to ignore and my athletic ability began turning heads. That's when expectations arrived almost overnight.

Suddenly, I wasn't just a child anymore. I was the one people pointed to when they needed reassurance that the chaos hadn't ruined everything. The one who would go somewhere. The one who would prove the struggle hadn't been for nothing. The pressure came wrapped in praise, and I didn't yet know how to refuse it.

Even then, before I understood faith as anything formal or intentional, there was a quiet sense of being watched over. Not in a dramatic way. Just a steady awareness that I wasn't completely alone in it all. Church with my grandparents had planted something early. It offered scripture, prayer, and a God who noticed the overlooked. Sometimes, I used to walk to church by myself just to sit in His presence. I didn't yet know how to name it, but I carried the sense that someone beyond the room was paying attention, even when the people in it weren't.

When we moved to Phoenix during my junior year of high school, something felt different. On paper, it was just another relocation—another school, another boyfriend my mother brought into our lives, another adjustment Wil and I would have to make. Emotionally, however, it signaled something unfamiliar, a subtle but undeniable shift.

Dan, my mother's boyfriend at that time, was the first white man she had ever dated. Race wasn't the thing that stood out to me most. What stood out was how he showed up.

He was present. He worked. He cooked meals. He paid attention. And for the first time in a long while, the house didn't feel heavy all the time.

Dan was an archaeologist, a career I didn't understand back then and honestly thought sounded boring. But he had curiosity in him, the kind that makes a house feel bigger. He introduced us to new things, teaching us how to shoot bows and arrows in the backyard, coaching us on form and focus as though he already saw capacities in us, we had yet to discover. He took us camping in real tents, pitched under open sky, bonfires crackling into the night, smoke weaving itself into our clothes as stories drifted upward with the sparks.

The house had laughter. Dan also loved practical jokes, the kind that startled you first and made you laugh afterward, the kind that reminded you joy could exist without conditions.

One Halloween stands out more than any other.

It was 1987, and my mother made it clear: Wil and I were not to come home until midnight—on the dot. Our house sat alone at the top of a slight hill, which already gave it an eerie presence once the sun went down. Just after midnight, Wil and his friends pulled up in one car, and my friends and I arrived in another just behind them. It was spooky-dark, the kind of night where even your footsteps sound louder than they should.

When we all got out, we saw it.

A furry figure perched on the roof.

Most of us froze, trying to make sense of what we were seeing. Wil— always quick, always thinking—grabbed the water hose and sprayed the roof without hesitation. The roof turned slick instantly, and whoever it was slid right off.

That's when I panicked.

I took off running down the hill toward the main street, scared to death. Running for my life! Moments later, someone was chasing after me, laughing, calling my name. It was Dan, letting me know it had been him all along.

We walked back up the hill together, me breathless, him still laughing at his own success. But the fun wasn't over. He led us around to the back of the house, to the French doors leading to the dining room. The night air was thick and dark. When he pulled the doors open, smoke billowed out into the night, curling around us like something out of a movie.

And then my mother rose from the ground, dressed as the Bride of Frankenstein.

It was elaborate. Thoughtful. Perfectly executed. Our friends lost their minds. They thought it was the coolest thing they had ever seen. And for once, I wasn't bracing for embarrassment or disappointment. I was just there—laughing, wide-eyed, part of something fun and memorable for the right reasons.

That's one of the reasons Dan remains my favorite among all my mother's past relationships. Whatever else was complicated between my mother and me, he created a different atmosphere in that house. He made room for play. He made room for light.

Phoenix mattered for another reason, too: it was the first time Wil and I were finally in the same school. We were so close that people thought we were twins. There weren't many kids who looked like us, and sticking together felt instinctual. If I were sitting at a lunch table and my freshman brother walked over, I would make sure there was room for him. Always. Part of it was love. Part of it was protection. We had learned early that proximity to each other made the world feel less overwhelming.

It was also the first time either of us experienced anything resembling stability. I was able to be in the same school for two consecutive years. Wil was able to attend all four years of high school in the same place, the most stability either of us had ever known.

We lived in a middle-to-upper-middle-class neighborhood for the first time. We weren't at the bottom anymore, at least not on the outside. The house even had a guest house that became my room, my own space. As a teenager, that was gold.

But life still required everything I had.

Wil and I were both active in sports with practices, games, and tournaments filling our weeks. But there was no lunch money. No help with fees. No medical. No cushion to catch us if something went wrong.

So, I worked.

I was in school full-time, playing sports, and working twenty-five to thirty hours a week at Taco Bell. I worked so that Wil and I could buy lunch instead of bringing leftovers. I worked so he could have track shoes and basketball shoes. I worked so we wouldn't stand out in a well-to-do neighborhood where being poor felt like something people could smell on you.

Looking back, I should have been exhausted. By any reasonable measure, I was. But I don't remember feeling tired. I remember momentum. I remember constant motion. A typical day meant school, basketball practice, and then straight to work. Homework happened whenever it could, late at night, early morning, or, if I'm telling the truth, finished in the preceding class before the bell rang.

I didn't frame any of it as sacrifice. I framed it as necessity. Someone had to make it work. And apparently, that someone was me.

I remembered how it felt to be teased for being poor, how deeply those moments lodged themselves inside me, and I was determined he wouldn't carry that same weight if I could help it. I shielded him where I could, buying lunches, covering shoes, smoothing edges before they could cut him.

And I appreciated that the protectiveness ran both ways. Even as the younger sibling, Wil often tried to flex like the older one, stepping in, checking on me, watching out for me in ways that still show up today. We learned early how to protect each other, and we never stopped.

Family dynamics continued to shape me in quieter ways. My brother and I sometimes talk about the favoritism we felt growing up. From the outside, though my dad was a father of convenience (he made time for us when it suited him), it might have looked like my dad favored me. To me, it always felt more like a form of protection, the way some fathers soften around their daughters.

With my mother, it was the opposite. Wil was allowed to express himself freely. His emotions were met with patience; his frustrations were tolerated. I learned quickly that my feelings were inconvenient. Any attempt to voice pain, concern, or disagreement was met with scolding or dismissal.

So I stopped trying. I internalized everything and became self-contained.

Even when people compared us—my grades against his struggles—I blamed myself and worried Wil would resent me for it. Over time, I started to resent the comparison itself, the way achievement became a measure of worth. Wil was never the problem, and neither was I. But we were being pitted against each other, intentionally or not, and I hated it.

That's why the comparisons hurt so much. My shine cast a shadow I never wanted him to stand in. It wasn't fair, and I didn't know what to do about it.

Amid all of this, something else began to form; not a loud rebellion, but a quiet one.

I never did drugs. I never collapsed into obvious self-destruction. Instead, I learned to skim the edges of self-destruction, hovering close without surrendering to it. God's grace held me steady in ways I didn't yet have language for. Still, I was tired. Tired of always being perceived as doing the right thing, tired of being the example, tired of being visible only when I was exceptional.

I wanted to fit in. To blend. To exist without every room feeling like it came with a separate set of rules written just for me.

That's where alcohol entered, not as desire, but as acceptance. Not to the point of addiction, but enough to recast me as the party girl. I didn't like the taste, and I didn't crave it, but I learned quickly that drinking was the currency of belonging in certain spaces, especially among the wealthy, popular kids. Alcohol smoothed edges. It made you less noticeable, less questioned, less other.

I didn't drink to escape. I drank to belong.

It was another form of code-switching, another way to manage perception without disrupting performance. By day, I was the responsible one: student, athlete, and provider. In social spaces, I learned how to mirror what was expected just enough to pass. Control stayed intact, and control was everything.

At home, responsibility had already taken root. I looked after my brother. I handled school without reminders. I learned how to move through spaces quietly, how to read moods, how to avoid adding weight to rooms already heavy with tension. Adults praised this and called it maturity, strength, and independence. No one asked what it cost to be that composed.

At school, the pattern continued. Straight A's. Perfect attendance. Teachers trusted me instinctively because I didn't need managing. I followed the rules, met expectations, and exceeded them when necessary. Reliability became my currency. If I did everything right, maybe nothing would fall apart. If I stayed impressive, maybe I would stay safe.

Athletics reinforced the same lesson. Whether on the track or the basketball court, I understood my role and executed it. Show up. Train hard. Perform. Don't complain. Don't falter. Coaches trusted me because I didn't need supervision. Once again, this was celebrated. No one stopped to ask why a teenager was so comfortable carrying adult-level pressure.

Inside, though, something else was happening. I stopped expecting care. I stopped imagining rescue. I stopped believing someone might step in for me the way I stepped in for others. I trusted my competence more than anyone else's consistency. That kind of independence looks admirable from the outside. On the inside, it's lonely.

Faith was the one place where I didn't have to earn my worth. God didn't need me to hold everything together. He didn't require perfection or performance. He simply stayed—quiet, steady, present. I didn't yet understand how deeply I would come to rely on that presence. I only knew that in moments of prayer, church, and stillness, I could loosen my grip just enough to breathe.

Still, I kept carrying.

Responsibility had become my identity. Being "the one" shaped how others saw me and how I saw myself. It kept me safe, but it also trapped me inside expectations I never knowingly consented to. By adulthood, this role would evolve into something more polished—leadership, perfectionism, and overachievement.

I wasn't driven by control so much as by fear. The fear that if I ever loosened my grip, someone would see through me. Competence became my shield. Preparation, my proof. Staying one step ahead felt safer than admitting I didn't always believe I belonged. The same instincts that protected me as a child would later propel me forward and eventually exhaust me.

But that reckoning hadn't arrived yet.

For now, I was still the responsible one. The expected one. The one everyone believed would make it, even when it meant carrying more than my share, and even when it meant carrying the weight of decisions that were never mine to make.

CHAPTER FIVE: THE DAY I WALKED AWAY

By my junior and senior years, I had learned how to be excellent without being seen. Out of five hundred plus students in my class alone (1988), I was one of about dozen or so Black students.

On the basketball court, I was an all-conference level player. Strong. Disciplined. Relentless. I trained the way I did everything else in my life—quietly, seriously, and with a sense that effort was the only protection I had. Track had already taught me how to push past pain, how to keep running even when no one was watching. Basketball gave me something similar, but with a different language: teamwork, court vision, trust.

What it didn't give me was advocacy.

No counselor ever pulled me aside to talk about college as they did my classmates. No one asked about my goals or explained scholarships or recruiting. No one ever said, "You're university material." I didn't even realize that "college-bound student" was an identity available to someone like me. In my world, people survived. They worked. They hustled. Dreaming wasn't part of the curriculum.

When high school ended, I did what made sense with the information I had.

I went to a junior college in northern Arizona to play basketball.

I thrived there in all the ways I knew how. I worked harder than everyone else. Harder in practice. Harder in conditioning. Harder in preparation. My coach believed in me deeply—still says, decades later, that I was the hardest-working player he ever coached. I was on pace for a full scholarship to a university. Doors were opening. Momentum was real.

For the first time, my life felt like it was moving forward instead of sideways.

And then I got pregnant.

Lindsay's father was on the men's basketball team. We weren't a couple. There was no grand love story or dramatic unraveling, just two young people making choices without understanding the cost. I never told him I was pregnant. He didn't learn of her until she was about 16. They are very close now and that makes me happy for them both. She deserves that bond. And in my own way, I feel like a wrong was made right. But at that time, there was so much fear around my pregnancy, I just moved on instinct.

I knew immediately that telling my mother I was pregnant would change everything.

I also knew what she would say.

So instead of going home that summer, I left.

I boarded a plane and flew across the country to my Auntie-Mom, the woman who had been a steady presence in my life when, so few others were. She was in the Navy and stationed in Virginia at the time, and in her home, I found safety, quiet, and something I hadn't felt in a long time: permission to think.

I stayed with her through the summer, waiting until I passed my first trimester. I knew that once I crossed that threshold, abortion would no longer be an option. That wasn't a decision made out of fear or pressure. It was conviction. God was with me there. I just knew this was not a line I would cross.

When I finally called my mother to tell her I was pregnant, she didn't disappoint.

"Is it too late?" she asked.

And just like that, whatever fragile hope I still carried for her acceptance collapsed. Our relationship—already strained, already brittle—fractured further. I wasn't angry. I was resigned. I understood her disappointment wasn't about me. It was about her own life, her own regrets, and her own sense of loss. But understanding didn't make it hurt less.

After the summer, I went back to Phoenix for a couple of months to pack up and leave my mom's disapproving energy. I took a year off from college, and I returned to Clovis, back to my grandparents' house—the place that had always been a sanctuary. Once Lindsay was born, I realized I wanted desperately to finish school.

And my little brother stepped into a role no teenager should ever have to assume.

He became Uncle-Dad.

He fed her. Bathed her. Dressed her. Combed her hair. Played with her. He loved her in ways that were gentle, instinctive, and profound. Watching him with her was humbling. He never complained. Never questioned why this was his responsibility. He simply showed up.

I, on the other hand, was unraveling.

I went back to school in northern Arizona, but my heart wasn't there. For the first time in my life, I was failing academically. I was drinking too much. Partying too hard. Losing myself in distractions I once would have judged. I wasn't lazy or reckless, I was hollow. Everything that had once motivated me had shifted. I wanted to be with my daughter. I wanted to feel whole again.

So, I left college again.

I moved back to Clovis to care for Lindsay.

But something had changed there, too.

My grandmother—the woman who had once carried so much for us— no longer had the strength to do it again. I don't fault her for that. I think she was tired. Tired of the back and forth. Tired of saving us from choices that weren't hers. My Pops continued to help where he could, but the message was clear: it was time to stand on our own.

Wil, Lindsay, and I moved into a tiny, rundown one-bedroom ADU. No heat. No refrigerator. Eventually, Wil bartered for a stove and used the oven for warmth. I wasn't working. Wil became our provider.

The roles reversed completely.

He walked more than two miles each way in the snow to work at Burger King. He wasn't dressed for it. Didn't have proper shoes or coats. Mrs. Gardner often offered him a ride. Yet he always thanked her kindly and continued walking. He never complained. He just did what needed to be done. He brought home salads for Lindsay and me, so we'd have something to eat. We often ate once a day.

When that wasn't enough, I started stealing food from the grocery store.

There was no shame in it, only urgency. My daughter needed to eat. Nothing else mattered.

Wil saw the truth before I did. This wasn't sustainable. He made a decision that would alter his life forever: he joined the military so he could help take care of us.

This wasn't his dream. It wasn't his plan. But it was his love.

A debt I will never be able to repay.

We used to say to each other, "I hope I die first, because I don't think I could survive losing you." Even now, I know that hasn't changed. I know with certainty that I would never recover from losing my brother.

Before he left for basic training, we bounced again—this time into a rundown trailer with holes in the floor, mice, and roaches. It was horrifying. Wil left for the Air Force the day after Christmas in 1991, carrying guilt he didn't deserve. He was leaving us behind. But I didn't stay there long. I couldn't.

Shortly after he left, I returned to Phoenix.

Pregnant again.

This time, I made the hardest decision of my life.

I gave birth to a beautiful little girl. I placed my daughter for adoption.

There is no graceful way to write that sentence. No language that softens it. It was the most devastating and clarifying moment of my life. I realized then that I was standing at the edge of a generational pattern. A pattern I had inherited, one I had begun to repeat, one that would consume all three of us if I didn't stop it.

I made that choice not because I didn't love her.

I made it because my love demanded more than I could give her.

I needed to do better. Become better. For Lindsay. For the daughter I placed. For myself.

Once the adoption was complete, something in me settled—not in peace, but in resolve. I immediately enrolled in paralegal school and earned my associate degree. I showed up. I focused. I rebuilt.

Shortly after that, I stepped into corporate America.

Not healed.

Not whole.

But awake.

That was the moment everything changed.

Not because life got easier.

But because I finally understood that survival was no longer enough.

CHAPTER SIX: THE COST OF COMPETENCE

I was twenty-four when I stepped into my first real corporate role, and for the first time in my life, I didn't feel like I was running from something. I felt like I was arriving.

I had just finished paralegal school when I landed an Executive Assistant position supporting the Director of Maricopa Health System. He was a Black man, my first glimpse of someone who looked like me holding real authority in a professional setting. I didn't just see him in passing or through a glass wall. I worked beside him. I supported him. I watched how he moved through rooms where decisions got made.

It mattered in ways that reshaped how I saw power. Not because I needed him to "save" anything in me, but because my whole life up to that point had taught me to expect power to look like someone else. In real time, I saw proof that power didn't have to look the way I'd been taught it did.

I was proud. Deeply proud. For the first time, I had something solid, something no one could take from me.

That joy lasted six months.

He was offered a CEO role with a start-up healthcare plan in Los Angeles. I was happy for him, of course I was. But also clear-eyed about what his exit meant for me. And I was also heartbroken because I could feel what was coming for me. When he left, it became clear that the person stepping into his role did not want me there. The warmth was gone. The tone changed. The air in the room changed.

When the new person took over, I didn't ask for a meeting. I didn't plead my case. I had learned long ago: when a room tells you you're not wanted, you leave before it asks you to.

So, I used the one strategy that would become my lifeline in corporate

America: I leveraged my relationships.

I stayed in touch with my former boss, and one day I asked him directly if there were any roles in the company he was building. He didn't hesitate. He sent me a list of open positions, and there it was: Paralegal.

The salary was forty-five thousand dollars a year. As a single mother, that number felt like a miracle. A moving company packed our belongings, and Lindsay and I drove from Phoenix to Los Angeles in my used, white Mazda RX-7, just the two of us, headed toward a future I had no intention of losing.

I wasn't afraid of the work. The only fear I carried was the fear of going backward, back to Phoenix, or worse, back to Clovis. I had already paid too high a price to retreat. So I wasn't going to let it be for nothing.

Los Angeles felt like a different planet at first. It was bigger, faster, sharper, and it demanded presence. I knew instinctively that perception mattered here in a way I hadn't fully felt before. I didn't want anyone to hear my twang and decide I was a country bumpkin who didn't belong in the big city. I didn't want anyone to look at what I wore and decide I was unpolished. I didn't want them to read my background on my face.

So, I built an image.

I bought the clothes, the shoes, the hair extensions, and weaves that made me feel closer to what "professional" looked like in that world. I wasn't trying to be someone else. I was trying to be safe. Taken seriously. Protected from being underestimated before I even opened my mouth.

And my voice started changing too, intentionally, and strategically. I launched our company's Toast Master's program. My Southern twang softened. My cadence became more measured. I began adopting the polished language I heard around me, not because I thought the way I spoke was wrong, but because I understood the rules of the game.

Then I'd go home and switch back.

The moment I walked back into family spaces, the rules flipped. The same refinement I worked so hard to build could make people look at me sideways. I was teased for "trying to sound white," and I learned quickly that code-switching wasn't just something you did to fit into corporate spaces. Sometimes you did it to fit back into your own.

Suits out there. Pajamas at home. Two versions of me, both real, both necessary.

The company itself was a startup, which meant I wasn't just a paralegal. I was whatever was needed. Legal work. Operational tasks. Facilities issues. HR executions. Holiday events. Errands. Problem-solving that didn't fit neatly into anyone's job description. I quickly became indispensable, trusted beyond my title, accountable beyond my job description. And I took that seriously.

This is where my moniker was born long before anyone actually said it out loud: Swiss Army Knife.

In startups, the ones who get ahead can do more than one thing well. They fill gaps without fanfare. They turn chaos into teamwork.

I could do that in my sleep. I'd been trained for it since childhood.

We had major regulatory deadlines—Knox-Keene licensing, DDA filings—and we were small. Small and mighty, people liked to say. That phrase always sounds inspiring until you're the one doing what "mighty" requires.

Twice a week, my days began at eight in the morning and didn't end until the next. I worked until five, rushed to pick up Lindsay, fed her dinner, tucked her in, and left her with my boyfriend or a sitter. Then I drove back to the office and worked through the night until six a.m. I drove home just long enough to make Lindsay breakfast, get her dressed, take her to school, and then I went straight back to work for another full day.

This wasn't a phase. It wasn't occasional. It was sustained. Lasting almost 8 months.

I was putting in sixty hours a week—sometimes more—and that isn't an exaggeration. It's a fact. There are receipts. None of my colleagues were doing that. And I never told my boss.

Not because I wanted to be a martyr. Not because I didn't notice the difference.

I didn't say anything because I wasn't working for applause. I was working for stability. For forward motion. For a future that wouldn't unravel if I slowed down. I was building margin the only way I knew how—by outworking uncertainty.

Looking back, I should have been exhausted. By any reasonable measure, I was. But I don't remember fatigue the way people usually describe it. I remember being locked in. Wired. Focused. Driven by a quiet, relentless urgency: keep going—because stopping had consequences.

Because I had already given up too much to fail.

Because no one was coming to rescue us.

Even when I made it home, the door didn't close. Pajamas didn't mean rest back then. They meant switching uniforms. The work clothes came off, but the responsibility stayed on. The setting changed, but the posture didn't.

I wasn't burning out yet.

I was executing.

One of my favorite things to do after those overnight stretches wasn't to sleep. It was to sit on the floor in Lindsay's room and listen to her breathe before I woke her up. She was always curled up in her Little Mermaid blankets, peaceful, warm, and safe.

I would sit there, exhausted, and feel something in me settle.

And then there it was. The reminder of a little girl who wasn't there.

They were my why.

The silence in my life during that season was both loud and quiet. Loud in action because everything I couldn't say, I proved through output. Quiet in voice because there were moments when my silence should have been audible, when I should have advocated for myself, but I didn't. I couldn't. Not when it felt like everything depended on me holding steady.

My faith was there too, even if it wasn't polished or performative. God's presence wasn't always something I could articulate or outwardly claim, but I felt it like you feel a hand at your back when you're walking through something heavy.

One night, when Lindsay was around eight, life was pulling on me from every direction. We lived in a top-floor corner apartment overlooking Westchester Park and LAX. I had a dream that was so vivid it felt more like a visitation than a dream. I saw Jesus standing outside below our balcony, in the grassy area of the park, dressed in white. No words. No instructions. Just peace. A pure, steady peace that said without saying: you're going to be okay.

I woke up comforted in a way that still stays with me. Not because all my problems were solved. But because the presence was undeniable. I was going to be ok; I just needed to trust Him.

After eight years in healthcare, I knew one thing clearly: I didn't want to be typecast as a healthcare professional. I didn't want my identity to be confined to one lane, one industry, or one label. I found a headhunter and told him, "Find me something in anything but tech."

He didn't listen. Thank God.

He placed me in my first tech company, and that decision shifted the entire trajectory of my career in ways I still benefit from to this day. I wish I knew his name so I could thank him properly, because that move wasn't just professional. It was prophetic.

Tech moves fast. It demands adaptability. It lives in constant change.

And this was the first environment that felt like it kept pace with my nervous system. People were stressed by pivots and reorgs; I was built for them. I didn't realize it then, but my childhood had trained me for exactly this kind of world.

At one Tech Company, I did what I always did. I worked hard. I performed. I solved problems. And, as usual, I absorbed work that wasn't mine when layoffs happened, and roles evaporated. Then I was asked to take on managing third-party partners.

I was excited. Not because I needed more on my plate, but because it felt like advancement. My colleague had been making a commission from those relationships. So, when the responsibility landed with me, I assumed compensation would too.

It didn't.

I was expected to do my full job and take on the same relationships she had been compensated for—without commission. I didn't discover this casually. It became clear in almost insulting ways, as if they assumed I wouldn't notice or wouldn't challenge it.

But I noticed. And I spoke.

When I was "laid off."

They offered me a severance package of one week's salary for every year of service. I had given them far too many years, and they offered eight weeks of pay as if it were generous.

I declined.

I told them plainly that I would sue them for unfair wages. I didn't say it to be dramatic. I said it because I knew what was right. And I knew what was wrong.

In the end, I negotiated a generous compensation and full medical coverage for Lindsay and me for almost a year.

It was a win.

But it didn't feel like victory. It felt like clarity: they were comfortable doing me wrong, and they counted on my silence to make it easy. Speaking up took that wrong and made it right.

That was the first time I understood something that would become a theme in my career: competence doesn't protect you. Loyalty doesn't protect you. Value doesn't protect you.

And it was around then that I learned another truth that was harder to swallow: sometimes the very thing people praise you for is the thing they use to keep you in place.

That became unavoidable at another tech company.

I was in a meeting with the Head of HR and several others. She was new—about a week into her role—and I wanted to raise concerns about a legal matter I knew would become an issue later. I was calm. Direct. Focused. I tried to explain it once, then another way when she dismissed it. I wasn't emotional. I wasn't reactive. I was doing what professionals do: addressing a problem early so it doesn't become a crisis later.

She cut through my point and said, "I feel like you're getting angry about this."

That phrase hit like a slap, not because it was loud, but because it was familiar. The dreaded phrase Black women go out of their way to avoid. I felt my body tense immediately—shoulders tightening, stomach knotting—but my face stayed neutral.

I couldn't give her the satisfaction of seeing me react.

Colleagues in the room had worked with me for some time. I knew they understood I wasn't angry. But it didn't matter. The fact that she could so casually assign that emotion to me simply because I disagreed was its own warning.

And the most frustrating part was the irony: she was Head of HR. She should have understood the consequences of saying that to a Black woman. She should have understood that those words don't float in the air harmlessly. They have history. They have outcomes. They have consequences.

That seed had been planted in another tech company, where the message became even more personal.

I was consistently a top performer. I earned bonuses, received high ratings - top 5 every year, and was given so many spot awards, they had to make a stink about the same "people" being given so much acknowledgement. Predictably, I took on responsibilities beyond my job description because I was good at what I did and because I didn't know how to do it any other way.

But with all of these receipts, my manager refused to promote me.

She eventually said the quiet part out loud: she was worried that if she promoted me, she might not be able to find a suitable replacement.

I remember sitting with that sentence like it had weight. Not because it shocked me, but because it named what I had always felt in my body: my excellence was being used as a reason to stall me.

What she called making me indispensable didn't feel like security. It felt like containment. My growth was inconvenient to her comfort, and my ambition was treated as something she didn't need to account for. And the kicker was, she got promoted! And yes, I will say it. Her promotion was in part due to my efforts. She didn't get there by herself. And I really resented how she assumed I had no dreams beyond supporting hers. Gratitude was the currency she expected in return for reliance, and for far too long, I accepted it, mistaking being needed for being valued.

This was also the company where I started noticing patterns beyond my own experience.

It wasn't just me. Black and Brown people weren't being promoted. Compensation was disproportionate. Stock options were either smaller, uneven, or not offered at all. Because of the roles I held— because I wore so many hats—I had visibility others didn't.

And seeing it in black and white did something to me.

It made me angry. It made me sad. It made me feel helpless and culpable at the same time, because I was privy to information, I couldn't broadcast without breaking confidentiality and violating my own integrity. I couldn't "save" people the way I wanted to. But I also couldn't unsee what I saw.

Something started burning slowly inside me.

Not rage. Not rebellion. A slow, steady recognition that the system was not neutral. That opportunity wasn't always about merit. That some people were being managed, not developed.

That's when my thinking began shifting from "How do I succeed?" to "How can I survive this and still keep my dignity?"

I didn't have the platform yet. I didn't have the language yet. But the seed was planted: if I couldn't fix the system from where I sat, maybe I could at least help people learn how to navigate it without losing themselves.

I wish I had called her out. Even privately later. But in that moment, I did what I had been trained to do since I was six years old: I took it.

Suits and Pajamas, again.

In the Suit, I kept my face composed, my voice measured, and my posture professional. I held my dignity with both hands.

In the Pajamas, later, I carried the weight of what I couldn't say. The reality that even with competence, even with restraint, even with performance, there were still people who would see me through the oldest lens.

This was the early spark of a bigger truth I hadn't fully named yet.

I had become excellent at navigating systems. Excellent at adapting. Excellent at delivering.

But I was also becoming aware of how much of that excellence was performance—necessary performance, yes, but performance, nonetheless.

And I was starting to suspect something that would eventually become undeniable: leadership without authenticity is just performance. And performance, no matter how polished, always extracts a cost.

At the time, I didn't call it burnout. I didn't call it misalignment. I didn't call it a fracture between who I was and who I was being forced to present.

I just kept moving. I kept achieving. I kept providing.

But somewhere underneath all that motion, the bill was being written.

And eventually, it would come due.

CHAPTER SEVEN: THE FREEWAY WASN'T BUILT FOR ME

For a long time, I believed that if I just worked hard enough, stayed sharp enough, and adapted quickly enough, I would eventually merge into the flow. That's what I had always done. That's what survival had taught me. You learn the rules, you master the terrain, and you keep moving.

But corporate America isn't a meritocracy, the way it advertises itself to be. It's a freeway system, and not everyone enters from the same on-ramp.

Some people are born already cruising in the fast lane. Others are waved through toll booths without stopping. And then there are people like me—skilled, capable, proven—who are expected to build the road while driving on it, absorbing every pothole and delay without complaint.

I didn't see it all at once. I saw it in fragments. Patterns that repeated across companies, across leadership teams, across years. At first, I told myself not to personalize it. Then I told myself to be patient. Then I told myself I was lucky just to be there.

Eventually, I had to tell myself the truth.

I had a front-row seat to something I would later learn had a name: **complexion protection**.

I witnessed it firsthand. More than once.

There was a white male employee who was notorious for his behavior. Openly sexist. Casually racist. Comments delivered in meetings without hesitation, sometimes with a smirk, sometimes with the calculated pause of someone daring the room to challenge him. These weren't whispers in hallways or things said behind closed doors. They were declarations. Public. Repeated. Audible to employees at every level, including executives.

Nothing ever happened.

Leadership knew. HR knew. Complaints were made. Concerns were raised. And yet, year after year, the explanation remained the same: *That's just how he is.*

As if harm becomes harmless when it's familiar.

As if longevity or the amount of "revenue" this person brings sanctifies character.
As if proximity to power absolves accountability.

I didn't need anyone to explain to me what would have happened if a Black or Brown man behaved the same way. There is zero chance he would have retained his job, let alone continued to rise. The rules were not unclear. They were selectively enforced.

Then there was another white male, this one known for sexually harassing women. Women spoke about it openly among themselves because there was no safe place to report it without consequence. His behavior was treated like an inconvenience to manage rather than a violation to confront.

His reward?

Promotion.
Then another promotion.

Then another.

Watching that was more than frustrating. It was nauseating. Because it made visible something I had long sensed but tried not to name: the freeway has guardrails for some and open cliffs for others.

And it wasn't just about misconduct.

Another guardrail less traveled by folks like me is access.

Every company has favorites. Everyone knows who they are. The people who are ushered into rooms where decisions are made. The ones whose calendars are suddenly filled with "visibility opportunities." The ones whose roles seem to expand albeit inorganically, while others remain fixed, no matter how much value they create.

I watched this happen repeatedly.

Roles were created for certain people. Impressive titles draped over vague responsibilities. Compensation packages that raised eyebrows if you looked closely enough. Invitations to C-suite meetings that had nothing to do with their actual scope of work.

And what made it worse—what made it impossible to ignore— was that many of those elevated weren't equipped to carry what they'd been handed.

So, they came to me.

Quietly.
Behind the scenes.

Off the record.

They asked for help. Guidance. Execution. Language. Strategy. I gave it because that's what I had always done. Because I was competent. Because I was dependable. Because I had been trained my whole life to solve problems without demanding credit.

Only later would I see my work surface with someone else's name attached to it.

This wasn't speculation. It wasn't paranoia. I saw the evidence after the fact. I had others who witnessed it, too. But because I wasn't in the room when the credit was claimed, I couldn't call it out in real time. And by the time it reached me, the promotion had already been approved, the compensation adjusted, the narrative sealed.

They continued to climb.

They continued to be rewarded.

And I continued to be useful.

I wasn't invisible.

I was essential.

And that, I would learn, is not the same thing.

The freeway rewards proximity, not contribution. It rewards familiarity, not excellence. And once you understand that you realize why so many talented people are stuck managing exits that lead nowhere.

This awareness didn't make me bitter. It made me alert.

I began to notice how often Black and Brown employees were overrepresented in execution and underrepresented in leadership. How we were trusted with responsibility yet denied authority. How we were leaned on in moments of crisis but overlooked when it came time to distribute opportunity.

I saw how equity, compensation, and stock options were distributed with quiet precision, uneven by design. How some people were granted futures while others were expected to be grateful for stability. I was privy to information most people weren't because of the roles I held, the hats I wore, the rooms I had adjacent access to, but not direct access within.

And that proximity came with its own cost.

I felt complicit.

Again, I couldn't act without breaching confidentiality or my own integrity. But knowing what I knew—and staying silent— ignited a slow, relentless burn inside me. I started mentoring others quietly, teaching them how to advocate for themselves, how to document their work, how to defend their value before someone else claimed it. I didn't yet have the language for what I was doing. I only knew I couldn't unsee the pattern.

Still, I kept driving.

Because leaving the freeway without a map felt dangerous. Because I had a daughter to provide for. Because I had already given up too much to turn back. Because momentum had always been my safest posture.

I told myself that if I just stayed sharp enough, adaptable enough, indispensable enough, then the road would eventually open.

What I didn't yet understand was that no amount of skill can overcome a system designed to filter who advances and who maintains it.

This realization didn't break me. Not yet.

But it did something quieter, more insidious.

It forced me to carry the weight of knowing that my success was conditional. That my excellence could be leveraged without being rewarded. That my labor could be celebrated without being elevated.

And it made me tired in a way sleep didn't fix.

I didn't talk about this openly. I didn't rage. I didn't quit. I did what I had always done: I adjusted. I endured. I stayed strategic. I stayed composed.

Outwardly, I was thriving.

Inwardly, something had shifted.

Because once you realize the freeway wasn't built for you, every mile requires more vigilance. You're watching for exits, scanning for obstacles, calculating risk in ways others don't have to. You're not just driving; you're managing survival at speed.

And that kind of constant awareness takes a toll.

I didn't yet call it burnout.

I didn't yet call it grief.

I didn't yet call it injustice.

I just knew I was carrying more than my share again.

And I kept going because stopping still felt more dangerous than continuing.

But the body keeps its own record.

And soon, it would begin to speak louder than my discipline ever could.

That reckoning is where the next chapter begins.

CHAPTER EIGHT: INDISPENSABLE IS A TRAP!

Burnout didn't come from work alone.

It came from the way I could never walk away.

Around the same time my career was accelerating, I started coaching. What began as something small—something meant for connection—slowly became another place where my sense of responsibility took root and refused to loosen its grip.

It started with a co-ed third-grade basketball team at Westchester Park. That was my introduction to coaching Lindsay. I loved it instantly. Being on the court with her, watching her learn, grow, and compete gave us something special to experience. A shared rhythm. A language beyond words.

But it didn't take long for me to notice something that bothered me.

The boys rarely passed the ball to the girls. Not when the girls were open. Not when they were positioned perfectly.

Not even when they were the better shot. The girls ran just as hard, paid just as much attention, and showed up with the same enthusiasm. But once the game started, they disappeared. Not because they lacked skill, but because they were erased.

And it wasn't just one or two teams. It was every team in the league.

The dads had opinions. Lots of them. Many were convinced they could coach better, strategize better, and lead better. The girls learned early to shrink themselves on the court, to hesitate before calling for the ball. To lower their hands when they weren't chosen, to make room for someone else's confidence.

I remember the exact moment it stopped being about basketball for me. I stopped seeing plays and started seeing a pattern. Girls running hard but going unseen. Hands raised in confidence, then lowered in resignation.

Talent waiting to be recognized before it dared to assert itself.

Their right to take up space was being negotiated in real time, and they were losing the negotiation.

That wasn't something I wanted to coach around.

It wasn't something I could ignore because once I saw it, I couldn't unsee it.

I did what I always do when something feels wrong: I acted.

I approached the parents of the one or two girls on each team and asked if they would be interested in forming an all-girls team, one that would compete against the boys. They didn't hesitate. They loved the idea.

That was the moment the ember was lit.

I loved coaching those girls. They were young, curious, and coachable. They listened. They learned. They trusted. And without even realizing it, I was building something much bigger than a basketball team.

For Lindsay, it became an adjacent sisterhood, one that would shape her confidence and identity in ways I couldn't yet see. For me, it became another place where I felt needed. Another place where leaving felt unthinkable.

After just one short season of hard work, the girls got good. Really good. They weren't just competitive. They were dominant. They started beating the boys, often decisively. Winning became routine. And with it came something far more powerful than trophies—confidence.

The dads were furious and frothing at the mouths demanding their boys play harder. As if losing to girls was the ultimate insult to their budding masculinity. I remember a particular time when a coach-dad yelled at his point guard son to "force them to the left". His natural assumption was that my girls were only right hand dominant.

I specifically called out to my point guard to run the play to the left, and the result was the same. Two points scored! The boy looked to his dad with the same "now what" expression. It was beautiful.

It was also a valuable lesson for both the girls and the boys alike. Don't underestimate the power of girls. Don't do it.

And then came the attention.

A private high school athletic director in Santa Monica took notice, and before I fully understood what was happening, I found myself offered the head coaching position for their varsity team.

I said yes.

Of course, I did.

I didn't stop coaching the younger girls. I couldn't. Instead, that team evolved into a travel team, competing across Los Angeles and Orange Counties. Different gyms. Different weekends. Different demands.

My calendar stopped being a calendar. It became a grid.

Monday, Wednesday, Friday: I dropped Lindsay off at school around seven in the morning. Worked from seven-thirty to two-thirty. Drove straight to the high school and coached varsity from three-thirty to five-thirty. Rushed to pick up Lindsay, fed her dinner, and spent time with her. Once she was settled and sometimes asleep, I logged back into work.

Deadlines were never missed. Tasks were always completed. No one complained because I made sure there was nothing to complain about.

On Tuesdays and/or Thursdays, the younger team practiced. Saturdays and Sundays were games. If varsity games conflicted, I rescheduled youth practices. I showed up everywhere.

I did this for almost five years.

Consecutively.

There's a particular kind of silence that settles in when you're doing too much for too long. Not quiet, just thin. As if the air itself has been stretched. I didn't notice it then. I just kept moving through it.

I told myself I was busy. Just committed. Just disciplined.

But the truth was more complicated.

I carried regret I never fully spoke aloud. The regret of the daughter I had placed for adoption, the ache of having walked away from her. That loss lived quietly inside me, shaping decisions I didn't always interrogate. Layered on top of that was the memory of my own mother walking away, of what it felt like to be left behind.

I didn't want any of those girls to ever wonder if they mattered. If they were worth my time. If they had been abandoned once they became inconvenient.

Some of the varsity girls had been kicked out of their homes for being gay. They slept on my couch. Others came from households marked by addiction or abuse. For some, basketball was the only place where they felt safe. It was the one place where they weren't judged. Where someone showed up consistently for them.

I was careful never to cross lines. I didn't speak badly about their parents. I didn't try to replace anyone. I was always clear that I was their coach.

But I made something else clear through my actions: they could count on me.

And once people learn they can count on you, leaving starts to feel like betrayal.

So, I stayed.

Even when I was weary.

Even when I was stretched thin.

Even when my life became nothing but work, parenting, and coaching.

There was no space left for rest.

No room for stillness.

No margin for myself.

I told myself this was purpose. That this was impact. That this was strength.

I didn't yet see that I was reenacting an old pattern, earning belonging through endurance, proving worth through self-sacrifice, and mistaking depletion for devotion.

Burnout doesn't always come all at once. Sometimes it builds quietly—layer by layer—when a person with unfinished grief keeps volunteering to carry more.

By then, my body had begun registering what my mind refused to acknowledge. I woke up tired in a way that felt cellular. Even sleep couldn't fix it. My shoulders often felt tight for no obvious reason, my thoughts buzzing long before my feet ever touched the floor. I moved through my days with precision, but there were moments when I felt strangely distant from myself, as if I were executing a role instead of living a life.

I called it focus.

I called it discipline.

I didn't yet have language for what it really was: depletion quietly taking root.

What unsettled me most was how familiar it felt. I had lived this rhythm before—absorbing pressure without complaint, staying useful to stay safe, moving fast enough that no one noticed how much I was carrying. As a child, that instinct had kept me invisible. As an adult, it made me indispensable.

Indispensable is a dangerous place to live. It's a trap.

Because the more indispensable you become, the harder it is to imagine stepping away. Rest starts to feel selfish. Setting something down feels like failure. You convince yourself that holding everything together is the same thing as living well.

Even my prayers had become transactional—quick asks whispered between obligations.

Help me get through this meeting.

Help me make this deadline.

Help me have the energy to show up one more time.

I still believed. I still trusted. But I no longer lingered. Faith, like everything else, had been folded into efficiency.

I thought this was just a season.

I didn't yet realize it was a pattern.

I didn't call it burnout.

I didn't call it grief.

I didn't call it injustice.

I just knew I was carrying more than my share again.

And I kept going because stopping still felt more dangerous than continuing.

But the body keeps its own record.

And soon, it would begin to speak louder than my discipline ever could.

That reckoning is where the next chapter begins.

CHAPTER NINE: THE MIRROR CRACKS

The mirror didn't shatter all at once.

There was no single moment where everything collapsed or came undone in some dramatic way. No crash. No breakdown. No headline-worthy crisis. What happened instead was quieter and far more dangerous. The mirror cracked slowly, almost imperceptibly, until one day I realized I could no longer recognize the woman staring back at me.

I had done everything I was supposed to do. Built a career. Provided for my daughter. Showed up. Delivered. Protected. Endured. From the outside, my life looked solid, even enviable. I was accomplished. Respected. Reliable. The kind of woman people described as "strong" without ever asking what that strength was costing me.

But inside, something had begun to loosen.

I didn't feel broken. I felt hollow.

I moved through my days efficiently, but without softness. I smiled easily, but rarely laughed from my gut. I handled problems quickly and decisively, without emotion, until emotion began surfacing in places I didn't expect. A sudden wave of sadness that made no sense. Irritation that felt disproportionate to the moment. Fatigue that sleep didn't touch.

What frightened me most wasn't the exhaustion.

It was the numbness.

I had lived so long in survival mode that I had mistaken functioning for flourishing. I knew how to push through. I knew how to manage chaos. I knew how to perform competently even when I was running on fumes. No one had ever taught me how to stop.

There were moments when I caught my reflection unexpectedly. In a bathroom mirror. In the darkened glass of an office window. I would pause, not because I disliked what I saw, but because I couldn't quite locate myself in it. Somewhere between lifelong pursuits of excellence, being the one who never wanted to disappoint, sitting in rooms where I wasn't fully seen or valued, and being the person, my family turned to whenever something fell apart. Whether death or crisis, I had lost clarity about who I was beneath the motion. I hadn't paused long enough to sit with myself to understand what mattered to me or what I wanted. Let alone answer it.

The mirror began breaking not because something new entered my life, but because something old finally demanded to be seen.

Patterns I had long normalized started showing up with uncomfortable clarity. The way I overextended myself. The way I tied my worth to usefulness. The way I felt safest when I was needed and most uneasy when I wasn't. The way I avoided stillness because stillness asked questions, I wasn't sure I was ready to answer.

I had built a life that rewarded endurance. But endurance, I was beginning to understand, is not the same thing as healing.

For most of my life, competence had been my armor. I wore it instinctively. Sharpened skills. Flawless execution. Anticipation before instruction. It protected me. It also concealed me. I learned early that excellence could keep me safe, even when it did not grant me access. And so, I stayed polished, prepared, precise, all while knowing that my competency alone would never be the key to the room.

Composure became another form of survival.

As a Black woman, my calm was never neutral. It was monitored. Assessed. Interpreted. Any deviation is scrutinized as evidence. My tone, my facial expressions, and my restraint all felt under constant surveillance. It was invisible labor, but it was heavy. And I carried it without ever naming it.

It was around this time that therapy entered my life. While it didn't offer instant relief, it offered a mirror I couldn't look away from. I didn't go because everything had fallen apart. I went because I was tired of holding everything together without understanding why.

For the first time, I saw how deeply my childhood had shaped my adulthood. Not just the pain, but the patterns. I saw how my drive, my excellence, my relentless self-reliance had been forged in environments where safety was conditional. Where love felt inconsistent. Where disappearing felt smarter than demanding.

Control had never been security. It had been fear in disguise.

Sitting across from someone who wasn't impressed by my competence or distracted by my accomplishments, I began tracing lines I had never fully connected before. Not because the events were unfamiliar, but because I had never allowed myself to see how deeply they spoke to one another.

What I remember most about that first session wasn't revelation. It was discomfort. The room felt too quiet. The couch was firmer than I expected, offering no place to sink or hide. My hands stayed folded in my lap as if they needed instructions. I wasn't sure how to begin, or if I even knew how to be vulnerable with a stranger.

All I knew was this. Whatever I had been doing to hold my life together was no longer enough.

One of the first truths to surface was the impact of placing my daughter for adoption. I had always framed that decision as strength. As sacrifice. As proof that I could do the hardest thing if it meant a better future. And in many ways, that was true. But counseling gave me permission to look beneath the bravery and name what else lived there.

Grief.

Not the kind that announces itself loudly, but the kind that settles quietly and rearranges your life from the inside. The kind that teaches you to overperform, so the loss won't feel wasted. The kind that convinces you that love must always be earned, never assumed.

I began to see how that loss had reinforced something already familiar. The belief that walking away, even when necessary, leaves a mark. That survival often demands sacrifice. That attachment is dangerous because it can be taken from you without warning.

That belief didn't start with adoption.

It started with my parents.

With a mother whose presence was inconsistent and whose resentment showed up in ways I didn't have language for as a child. With a father whose absence taught me early that love wasn't something I could rely on. With the quiet understanding that if I wanted to be chosen, I needed to be exceptional.

Counseling helped me see how those early lessons shaped everything that came after.

My drive for perfection wasn't ambition. It was adaptation.

My need for acceptance wasn't insecurity. It was survival.

My exhaustion wasn't accidental. It was cumulative.

I had spent years trying to outrun the feeling of being unseen by making myself undeniable. Straight A's. Athletic excellence. Corporate success. Leadership. Reliability. I believed that if I became impressive enough, indispensable enough, I would finally be safe from abandonment.

The mirror didn't just show me who I was.

It showed me why.

And that clarity was both devastating and liberating.

Because once I understood the origin of my patterns, I could stop judging myself for them. I could honor the younger versions of me who did the best they could with what they had. And I could finally begin the work of choosing differently, not from fear, but from truth.

Faith, too, began to change shape.

God had always been present in my life. I knew that. I had felt His protection in ways I couldn't explain. Doors that opened when they shouldn't have. Moments where I was spared consequences I probably deserved. But somewhere along the way, my relationship with Him had narrowed. Faith had become functional. Supportive, but distant. Reliable, but restrained.

Healing brought Him closer again.

Not as a taskmaster.

Not as a safety net.

But as a companion.

I began to understand that God had not just been preserving me. He had been preparing me. That the very things I once believed disqualified me were the same things shaping my purpose. That my story wasn't something to outrun or reframe. It was something to integrate.

The mirror broke when I finally allowed myself to see all of it at once.

The child who learned to disappear.

The teenager who learned to perform.

The woman who learned to lead.

None of them was wrong. None of them was weak. They had all done exactly what they needed to do to survive.

But survival was no longer enough.

What followed wasn't resolution. It wasn't peace. Not yet. It was awareness. And awareness, I learned, is both a gift and a burden. Once you see yourself clearly, you can't pretend you don't. Once the mirror cracks, you can't unsee the reflection.

This was the beginning of my reckoning. Not with the world, but with myself.

And it would require something far more difficult than endurance.

It would require surrender.

CHAPTER TEN: GRIEVING A MOTHER STILL LIVING

The mirror didn't finish breaking in the last chapter. It cracked just enough to show me where to look next.

Awareness has a way of redirecting your gaze, whether you're ready or not. Once you understand that the patterns in your life didn't appear randomly, you start tracing them back to their source. You see them through choices, through relationships, through memories you've spent years skimming past because stopping felt too dangerous.

When I followed my patterns far enough, they all led to the same place.

My mother.

Not as a caricature. Not as a villain. Not even as the person she became in my adulthood. But as the original relationship where love, survival, resentment, and expectation first collided.

For most of my life, I described our relationship as complicated. That word gave me room to breathe without telling the whole truth. It softened the edges. It excused the contradictions. It allowed me to keep hoping without naming how often hope had been used against me.

But once the mirror cracked, that word stopped protecting me.

What I was seeing in myself had an origin. And it wasn't abstract. It was relational.

The truth was brutal in its simplicity.

I had been waiting for a mother who did not exist.

The first crack came when I was fifteen, living in Spring Valley.

I had a crush on a boy at school, the kind of crush that makes everything feel heightened and fragile. He was popular, kind to me, and impossibly handsome in the way only teenage infatuation can make someone seem. I still remember his birthday.

One evening, I was babysitting two neighborhood kids when the phone rang. A voice on the other end said his name. My heart jumped. He told me he liked me. Asked if I wanted to go on a date.

I didn't question how he got the number. I was too naive. Too hopeful.

I said yes.

Then the laughter exploded.

Sharp. Loud. Unrestrained.

It was my mother and her new twenty-one-year-old husband "pranking" me.

I stood there frozen, phone pressed to my ear, as they laughed at me— at my excitement, my vulnerability, my belief that someone could want me. There was no explanation. No "just kidding." No apology. Just amusement at my expense. And they hung up.

Something in me shut down that night. Not anger. Not defiance.

Withdrawal.

The following year, we were back in Clovis, and I was invited to a military ball. My mother let me wear one of her dresses. It was my favorite. A lavender gown, fitted and elegant, brushing the floor. I remember how carefully I got ready, how beautiful I felt, how badly I wanted her to tell me how pretty I looked.

She looked me over once and said casually, without warmth, "That dress looks better on me."

The words landed cleanly, sharply, and stayed with me for years. I learned then that my beauty was something she wanted to compete with, not celebrate.

When I was twenty-two, living in Phoenix and attending paralegal school, I experienced something I had never known before: a Black professor. He was young, intelligent, and confident. I developed a harmless crush—private, unspoken, safely contained within the pages of my journal.

That journal was mine.

Sacred.
Private.

My mother read it.

Then she called him.

I found out when he pulled me aside after class, visibly uncomfortable, and told me about the call. I wanted to disappear. I still had to sit in his classroom every day, carrying the humiliation of being exposed.

My mother never explained why she did it.

She never apologized.

By the time I became a mother myself, the pattern was clear, and I was done repeating it.

One winter afternoon, my mother was driving with my daughter— only three at the time—sitting in the back seat. The windows were up. She lit a cigarette. I had asked her many times not to smoke around Lindsay. She had just had bronchitis months earlier, and I was worried.

When I asked her again to stop, she exploded. She told me it was her car, she was grown, and she could do whatever she wanted.

I told her she was choosing a habit over her granddaughter's health.

I told her to pull over.

I took my daughter out of the car and walked home, carrying her nearly two and a half miles without looking back.

That was the day I became the mother I never had.

Years later, everything changed in 2012.

What died wasn't the relationship itself. It didn't come during our loudest fight. It didn't come during one of the many arguments where voices were raised, and history rewritten.

It came quietly, the moment I stopped reaching for her at all.

In that moment, something very specific died.

Not love.

Not obligation.

Hope.

That she would soften. That time would heal. That if I tried harder, loved smarter, succeeded louder, she might finally see me.

I was driving home from work during my three-hour commute, returning calls as I always did. My mother and I got into an argument—one of many—but this one was different. Her words were sharp. Deliberate.

She told me she didn't like me.

She told me she would never respect me.

And for the first time, something in me went still.

That's when I officially grieved the loss of my mother.

Before hanging up, I told her something I had never said aloud until that moment. I told her that one day she would need me. That she had no savings, no plan, and no safety net. And that when that day came, I would be there. Not because she deserved it. Not because she had earned it.

But because God required it of me.

I wasn't going to stand before Him, having failed to do what was right.

I ended the call knowing—without bitterness, without drama—that there was no longer a future where I had a mother-daughter relationship in any meaningful sense of the word. And so, I grieved her that day. Not because she was gone, but because of the possibility of who she could have been to me.

From that day forward, our relationship became transactional. Clear. Boundaries.

It was the same role I had learned early—do what is required, expect nothing back, and keep moving.

I detached without hatred. I stopped explaining. I stopped hoping.

And the relief was immediate.

Understanding her came later.

My mother was the eldest of six children—three girls, three boys—born into a structure that assigned responsibility before consent. She grew up in deep poverty. Dirt floors. Outhouses. Cotton fields starting at age seven. She was parentified early, carrying burdens far too heavy for a child.

Love in her home was not expressed. It was enforced. Discipline came by way of belts, tree switches, and cable cords. Children were noticed most when they were in trouble.

She never learned how to be gentle.

She never learned how to rest.

When she became pregnant at seventeen, her life didn't pause. It collapsed forward. She was still a child herself, suddenly responsible for three children by the age of twenty-one.

She couldn't give what she had never received.

Knowing that didn't excuse the harm, but it gave it context. And space to feel empathy without betraying myself.

The conflict between us was never love versus cruelty. It was survival mistaken for motherhood. Control mistaken for care. Resentment mistaken for authority.

I was living proof of the life she never got to have. And I think some part of her never forgave me for that.

By 2012, the truth had become unavoidable.

Forgiveness, I learned, is not absolution. It is freedom.

It freed me to mother my own daughter differently; to listen, to repair, to cherish, to protect and love without resentment. Loving her exposed what I never received, but it also showed me what was possible.

Faith held me through that reckoning. Not loudly. Not theatrically. Just steadily.

God didn't erase the pain. He gave me the strength to carry it honestly.

I hold my mother with distance. With compassion shaped by clarity. I expect nothing from her now, and because of that, I am free.

I care for her because it is right.

Because God asked me to.

Because I refuse to let bitterness inherit my future.

I didn't know then how literal that promise would become. I only knew I had made it.

When she leaves this world, I will know I honored her without abandoning myself.

That is the legacy I choose.

And that choice—quiet, firm, unromantic—is how generational trauma ends.

CHAPTER ELEVEN: A FATHER AT THE EDGE OF THE FRAME

The earliest memory I have of my father after my parents' divorce is not a visit or a conversation. It is punishment.

I was still a little girl when I stole a piece of candy from the local Allsups convenience store. My mother caught me and made me return it. That should have been the end of it. But my father, who lived more than an hour away and whom we rarely saw, decided to drive to our apartment to teach me a lesson. He whipped me severely. I don't remember him visiting us before that. I don't remember him sitting with us, asking questions, or staying long enough to be known. What I remember is discipline without presence.

He lived an hour away, but it might as well have been another world. We saw him once or twice a year at most. He was a man of the streets, known throughout West Texas and Eastern New Mexico. His name carried weight. Fear, even. His life reflected decades of drinking, violence, and gambling. That reputation followed him everywhere. Including into our lives.

One moment stands out when I was about ten, and my brother was eight. On one of his rare visits, our dad picked us up in Clovis and drove us to Amarillo. He told us we were going to Wonderland, a small amusement park. We were ecstatic. I was always the daredevil, eager for the biggest, fastest rides. But instead of going inside, he parked just outside the entrance and began playing craps. He lost all the money. We never went in. We stood there, two kids staring through the fence at the rides we could almost touch. I remember crying. Then I remember getting angry. Not just for myself, but for my brother. That was the moment I decided I could never trust anything my father promised.

I was a daddy's girl by nature. Most girls are, until reality hits. Mine hit early.

What's important to understand is that I didn't spend my adult life explaining my father away or softening his absence for others. I did the opposite. I rarely spoke about him at all. How do you explain a relationship you never truly had? I grew up in an era where parents were automatically expected to be revered and children, regardless of age, were supposed to accept whatever was given. My father operated from that assumption. He believed he could come and go as he pleased simply because he was the dad. I resented that entitlement and responded by keeping him at a distance. Proximity implies relationship, and he hadn't earned that with me. Over time, silence became my boundary. Not out of spite, but out of clarity. He slowly disappeared from my narrative because, for most of my life, he had never really been in it.

That early unreliability shaped me in ways I didn't yet have language for. I learned to expect very little from men. I learned to rely on myself. I learned that love could be intermittent and still demand loyalty. I adapted to having two absent parents in different ways: my father physically, my mother emotionally. And I tolerated this inconsistency because it was familiar.

The turning point didn't come through forgiveness or understanding. It came through confrontation.

Lindsay was a newborn when I invited my father to visit us in Clovis. He lived in Amarillo at the time. I wanted him to spend time with us. I wanted to see if something could be different. I extended the olive branch to give him an opportunity to build a loving, present relationship with Lindsay.

He arrived late Friday afternoon. By eight that evening, he was gone, out clubbing with his friends. He returned around two in the morning, ready to sleep it off. The next day, he woke late, had breakfast, and left again. I waited for him to come back to spend time together. He didn't. Saturday night mirrored Friday. When he returned at two in the morning, I had had enough.

I had taken all of his belongings and thrown them off the second-story balcony. Every last thing. I did not open the door. He pounded and yelled, demanding to be let in. I didn't move. I told him he could go stay with his friends, since they clearly mattered more. Later, I told him the truth: he failed as a father. He had never been there. And I would never let my daughter suffer the same. I told him he had failed me, but he still had an opportunity to be a good grandfather.

That moment didn't transform him overnight. But it did change something. Over time, my father became a wonderful grandparent to Lindsay, showing up for her in ways he never did for me. And strangely enough, that was enough. I am grateful she received the best of what both my parents were capable of giving, even if that version only arrived with age and distance.

Today, my father and I have a healthy relationship. It will never be what I hoped for as a little girl, but it is real. I know he loves me. And I love him very much. I know he would do anything for my brother and me now. I also know that he became a father before he had the capacity to understand what that meant. Like my mother, he did the best he could with what he had. And like my mother, the consequences of that shaped me profoundly.

I didn't know I was carrying that wound.

I only knew what it felt like when it finally wasn't there.

CHAPTER TWELVE: LETTING IN A LOVE THAT STAYED

I didn't walk into my relationship with David looking to be saved.

By the time I was ready to put myself out there, I had already made peace with what I would never receive from my parents. Not in a dramatic way. Not with bitterness. Just with clarity. I had stopped waiting for people to become who they had shown me they could not be. And in that letting go, something important shifted.

I wasn't hungry for love anymore.

I was available for it.

That distinction mattered.

For most of my life, connection had always come tangled with instability. Love arrived inconsistently. It demanded adjustment. It required vigilance. I learned early how to accommodate absence, how to lower expectations, how to keep moving even when something essential was missing. I didn't know how deeply that shaped my relationships until it stopped shaping them.

After confronting the truth about my father and releasing the fantasy of a different kind of mother, I became more intentional about who I allowed into my life. Especially where my daughter was concerned. Lindsay was eighteen now and she had already lived through enough transitions that weren't hers to choose. I was determined that the people closest to her would be rooted, present, and accountable.

That resolve didn't make me closed off.

It made me discerning.

When I met David, it wasn't from a place of longing or restlessness. It came from a season of steadiness. My life was full. My days were structured. My responsibilities were clear. I wasn't searching for distraction or drama. I wasn't trying to fill a void. I was simply open to companionship, if it showed up with integrity.

I didn't know then that David would become my husband. I didn't know he would become family. What I knew, almost immediately, was that being with him didn't require me to brace myself. I didn't feel the familiar tightening in my chest, the quiet calculation of what might go wrong, the need to stay one step ahead emotionally.

For the first time, connection didn't ask me to perform.

It simply asked me to show up.

That was new.

And it changed everything.

Back then, online dating still carried a certain stigma. It felt impersonal and uncertain, like handing your heart to an algorithm and hoping it didn't mishandle it. The truth was the traditional ways of meeting men no longer fit my life. I didn't go out much. My days were full. Work. Parenting. Coaching. Responsibility layered on responsibility. If I were going to meet someone, it would have to happen differently.

I took a leap of faith.

I was about to turn thirty-eight. David was just shy of fifty. We came from different worlds in almost every measurable way. I'm Black. He's White. I'm the eldest, shaped by responsibility from an early age. He's the baby of five, raised in a home where stability wasn't something you hoped for. It was simply there.

He grew up in the same house his entire childhood in Inglewood, California. Two loving parents who stayed together until his father died in the mid-1980s. Four siblings who shared history, memory, and continuity. I grew up in motion. Eleven schools. Multiple states. Adults who came and went. Permanence that always felt provisional.

And yet, from the beginning, there was ease.

Our first date didn't feel performative. It felt spacious.

We started with sushi. Simple. Unpretentious. Then we drove to Vasquez Rocks in Agua Dulce, California. The landscape opened up around us, wide and quiet, ancient in a way that made time feel less urgent. We talked for hours. Not the curated kind of conversation meant to impress, but the kind that wanders through childhood, work, loss, humor, and belief.

Nothing felt rushed.

Nothing felt forced.

That night didn't convince me he was "the one." What it did show me was something I hadn't realized I was missing: presence without pressure.

David's life experience was different from mine in other ways that were immediately apparent. I worked in corporate America, fast-paced, political, and constantly shifting. He had built what would end up being a forty-one-year career at Amtrak, starting as a train crew member and working his way up to emergency manager. His career was rooted in consistency, process, and long-term trust. Mine had been shaped by adaptability, vigilance, and navigating systems not designed for me.

We learned early not to treat those differences as obstacles.

They became a classroom.

I was serious, always in go-mode, carrying responsibility like a second skin. David was more measured. He paused. He breathed. He didn't equate urgency with importance. Instead of frustrating me, that steadiness began to soften something in me.

He wasn't trying to slow me down.

He wasn't trying to change me.

He was showing me another way to move.

This was my first marriage. It was his third. That difference mattered.

David had already lived through the unraveling of relationships. He understood that love isn't sustained by intention alone. It requires compromise, repair, and humility. I was learning those things in real time, unlearning the instinct to retreat when conflict surfaced, to self-contain instead of engaging.

One of our earliest challenges came through step-parenting.

David had two children from his first marriage. Lindsay fit right between them in age. Because of my own history with stepfathers who were largely absent or indifferent, I didn't want to hover at the edges. I wanted to step in. To show up. To care. To be available.

But blended families don't move in straight lines. David's children already had a mother. They had rhythms and loyalties formed long before me.

There were misunderstandings. Competing loyalties. Feelings that didn't always have language yet. Navigating those complexities required more than good intentions. It required David and me to have hard conversations early. To name discomfort without accusation. To prioritize our partnership even when the path felt unclear.

What anchored us was a shared commitment to a simple framework.

It was never me versus him, or him versus me.

It was always us versus the problem.

That mindset changed everything.

It allowed us to disagree without destabilizing the relationship. To acknowledge our different instincts without turning them into weapons. To build something rooted not in perfection, but in partnership.

What confirmed that David was different wasn't a grand declaration or a dramatic turning point. It was the way he loved my daughter.

From the beginning, there was no separation in his mind between loving me and loving Lindsay. There was nothing I ever wanted for her that he didn't support without hesitation. Her hopes became his hopes. Her future mattered to him not as an extension of me, but as its own sacred thing.

He respected her. He genuinely liked her. He was fiercely protective in a way that never felt performative or conditional.

That distinction mattered more to me than I can explain.

Years later, when Lindsay was living in New Orleans, she began dealing with a neighbor who was racist and relentlessly harassing her. When David found out, there was no debate. He got on a plane immediately.

He sat on her stoop. He waited. He confronted the man directly.

I wasn't there, but I know David well enough to understand how it unfolded. Calm. Direct. Intimidating. Unmistakable. The kind of confrontation that doesn't require raised voices to land. The man walked away shaken, fearful enough to call the police. Not because of theatrics, but because David made it clear that harm toward Lindsay would not be tolerated and there would be consequences.

Watching him step into that role did something to me. It healed a place I didn't know was still tender.

I had another moment like that earlier in our relationship.

We were at a restaurant in Oxnard, California. David had his back to a couple of men. I was facing them and immediately noticed the looks. The kind you learn to read quickly when you've lived in a Black body long enough. Disapproval. Judgment. Hostility thinly disguised as curiosity.

I didn't tell David.

Not because I didn't trust him, but because I trusted him too much. I knew that if he turned around and saw what I saw, he would confront them.

I didn't want to escalate something that could become dangerous.

Later, in a different conversation, he told me something I've never forgotten.

He said he knew I was a fighter. That I was built for confrontation, not retreat, because I'm a ride or die for my husband. If we were ever threatened, my instinct would be to stand my ground beside him.

Then he made me promise something.

If that moment ever came, if something truly went sideways, I had to run. I had to get away.

Not because he doubted my strength, but because he understood his role. As long as I stayed, his attention would be split. Protecting me would override everything else. But if I ran, he could fully handle the situation or get away if necessary.

That was the moment my body understood something my mind was still catching up to.

I had never felt so safe.

Not because nothing bad could happen, but because I knew someone else was watching the perimeter.

I had spent most of my life being my own protector.

Before David, there had only ever been one exception. My brother. He was the only person I had ever felt truly safe around, the only one whose presence quieted my vigilance instead of heightening it. We learned early how to guard each other, how to read danger without naming it, how to stand between harm and the people we loved.

Letting someone else step into that role felt unfamiliar.

With David, it didn't feel like surrender. It felt like trust being shared.

And that was transformative.

Over time, our life filled with memories that felt expansive. Camping trips. Long drives. Quiet mornings. And travel. Cancun. Italy. Amsterdam. Jamaica. London. Sydney. New Zealand. Spain. Before he met me, David had never been out of the country. Watching his face light up as he experienced the world has become one of my great joys.

At home, love showed up in quieter ways.

When I came home from long days at work, David met me at my car, took my briefcase, and kissed me hello. Every time. My colleagues didn't believe me, so I recorded it so they could see that yes, he's that guy. He also packed my breakfast and lunch because he knew I would forget. Sometimes I walked into the house and found a bath already drawn, steam rising, silence waiting.

These weren't grand gestures.

They were consistent ones.

Consistency, I learned, was what allowed me to trust again.

There is one place where our differences remain unresolved.

I believe in God. David does not.

I believe his experience in Christian-based schools from K-8th shaped a relationship with faith that left him unconvinced. For me, faith has been a constant thread. Quiet at times. Taken for granted at others. But always present. Not being able to share that spiritual connection with him has been difficult. It's a gap I still navigate.

And yet, respect lives there.

David doesn't diminish my faith. I don't try to convert his disbelief. We hold that difference honestly. It isn't perfect, but it's real.

Through God and through my marriage, I learned that healing doesn't happen in isolation.

It happens when someone stays long enough for your nervous system to recalibrate. When love doesn't require armor. When trust is built through presence, again and again.

David didn't rescue me.

He met me.

And in that meeting, I began to soften. Not into dependence, but into partnership.

For the first time, love didn't feel like something I had to manage.

It felt like something I could finally share.

CHAPTER THIRTEEN: WHEN MEMORY FADES, AND PEACE ARRIVES

There was no single moment when I realized my mother had Alzheimer's.

No dramatic scene.

No sudden collapse of recognition.

No doctor's office revelation that split my life neatly into *before* and *after*.

Instead, there was a slow undoing of the woman who once held all the power in our relationship and a quiet reversal that reshaped us both.

It came the way grief often does. Softly at first. Almost politely. And then undeniable the moment you stop pretending you don't see it.

In hindsight, the earliest signs had been building for years—we just hadn't said its name out loud. Around 2014 or 2015, my mother had begun isolating herself in her home in Phoenix. When I visited, she stayed holed up in her bedroom, door locked, curtains drawn, phone unanswered, the world reduced to a narrow radius she could control. She was depressed, though she would never have called it that. She had shingles—brought on, no doubt, by stress, shame, and the quiet humiliation of needing help while resenting the very people providing it.

I had spent my childhood trying to be seen by her. Now she was the one fading from view. This was not the woman I grew up with.

My mother had always been a social butterfly. She knew how to throw a party. How to gather people. How to be seen. But something in her had begun to dim. The zest for life she once carried so effortlessly was fading, replaced by suspicion, withdrawal, and an undercurrent of anger that none of us could quite place.

She started forgetting things that were once etched deeply into her memory, details so foundational that I felt each one slip away in real time. I wasn't trying to diagnose her. I didn't need to. I had seen this before.

My grandmother.

The same patterns.

The same confusion.

The same slow unraveling.

By 2019, David and I were living in Los Angeles, building a life we loved and planning a future that pointed toward Seattle. My mother, meanwhile, had moved to Florida to live with her sister, the woman I call my Auntie-Mom. They had never been particularly close. In fact, there was a deeply rooted resentment my mother carried toward her that had never healed.

I think it came from two places.

She resented my bond with her sister.

And she resented the way our family revered her.

My Auntie-Mom was cherished. Respected. Trusted. She had earned it through consistency, care, and presence. My mother watched that from a distance, and it hardened something in her.

Yet and still, my Auntie-Mom took my mom into her home to look after her sister. They lived next door to my brother, and as the tension between them grew, so did my certainty that something had to change. My mother's forgetfulness was no longer occasional. It was consistent. Concerning. It had taken a turn, indicating she was on the decline.

Then COVID arrived.

The world stopped, fractured, and reset itself in ways none of us were prepared for. And unexpectedly, it became the catalyst for what came next.

I had been planning my fiftieth birthday for months, a masquerade ball, casino tables, a live band, and a DJ. It was going to be extravagant. Intentional. And surprisingly, it was going to be my first birthday party ever. I was finally allowing myself something celebratory.

COVID canceled all of it.

That same spring, my twin nieces were graduating from high school in Florida. David and I were excited to gift a down payment on a car for each of them to celebrate this milestone. We flew out—masked, cautious, and uncertain but ready to celebrate.

What I saw during that trip changed everything.

My mother's health had declined noticeably. Her relationship with her sister was deteriorating fast. The tension in the house was thick. Unspoken. Volatile. And for the first time, I understood that distance was a luxury we no longer had. And that the time had come.

I had to have the discussion with David that our dream of moving to Seattle was no more and that I needed his support. It was during that trip that we pivoted our plans. So, while we were there, David and I decided—almost casually—to look at houses. Just reconnaissance. Just information.

After looking at several houses, we found a home we both loved. One that sat fifteen minutes from my brother's house. One that had a separate apartment over the garage just for mom.

It felt intentional.

It felt possible.

It felt terrifying.

Within two weeks, we closed.

On June 28, 2020, we moved to Florida.

Five weeks.

That's how long it took for everything to change.

In that span, we flew to Orlando, returned as homeowners, flew back to sign documents, packed up our three-story townhome in Los Angeles, hired movers, shipped our cars, and relocated across the country, while I continued working full-time.

I took two days off.

Two.

I don't know how I did it.

Actually, I do.

I was still trying to prove that I could carry everything without dropping anything. That I could be "on" no matter what. That my needs were secondary to my reliability.

My employer didn't overtly require me to stay "on," but I felt it all the same. I had never experienced unlimited PTO as something that applied to me. As a Black woman, I had learned that absence could be misread, that stepping away might cost more than it gave. I know now that this belief was learned, not law. I didn't feel free to disappear, even briefly. Not then. Not when reliability had always been my currency. Later in my life, I would eventually lay that fear down. At the time, I carried it like armor.

We chose that house because it gave my mother her own space and gave David and me boundaries. We invited her into our home, rent free. Nothing had changed between my mother and me emotionally. If anything, her resentment intensified. I think realizing she needed me unsettled her in ways nothing else ever had.

From 2020 to 2022, she remained relatively independent. I shared my red Dodge Charger with her since I worked from home. We paid for the insurance, maintenance, and gas. She ran errands. Bought groceries. Came and went as she pleased.

Until the night she didn't come home.

It was past seven. Then eight. Then later. My mother was never quick, but this was different. Months earlier, David had installed a tracker in the car, thinking ahead in a way I hadn't wanted to admit was necessary.

When we checked the tracker, she was more than an hour away, near Disney World.

We immediately left, following her signal the way you follow a fading star: not to catch it, but to keep it from disappearing entirely.

We found her at a gas station, asking for a phone charger because her phone had died. When she saw me walk through the doors, she broke down crying—overwhelmed, confused, relieved, and undone.

I was the one who found her.

The daughter she said she didn't like.

The daughter she said she'd never respect.

That night changed something.

Her ability to manage appointments, medications, and meals deteriorated quickly after that, but she still resisted help. Until she couldn't.

She had been a smoker her whole life. In the fall of 2022, she underwent bypass surgery due to severe blockage in her legs, compounded by a toe infection that she hid from me that landed her in the hospital for a week. When she was discharged, she required round-the-clock care.

And just like that, David and I became the care team.

Even after that harrowing surgery, she continued smoking. That decision alone led to another bypass less than a year later. Another hospital stay. Another stretch of me working from my laptop at her bedside, taking calls in hallways and parking lots, toggling between crisis management at work and crisis prevention at home.

When clotting followed the second surgery, we had yet another hospital stay. This one was briefer, but there I was yet again. Working from my laptop at her bedside, taking calls in hallways and parking lots. At this point, I was done, and I took the car keys. As long as she had them and was driving, she was going to buy cigarettes.

That was the line.

Aside from denying her access to the thing she craved, she was no longer safe to drive. She fought me. Made my life miserable. Said terrible things. But I didn't waver. And in taking her keys, something unexpected happened.

She was no longer smoking.

Just like that.

She hasn't had a cigarette since 2023. And she hasn't required another bypass either. That decision gave her more time on this earth. I know it did.

All of this unfolded while I was leading global M&A integration efforts—traveling internationally, securing coverage, coordinating care. Sometimes David stayed behind to care for my mother. Sometimes my aunts and uncle rotated in to help. For six years, my life has been a constant negotiation between responsibility and presence.

But here is the truth.

I obeyed God.

I did what He asked of me.

Whether my mother deserved my consideration was never the question. My obedience was between God and me. And years ago, He made it clear that I would be the one to care for her. Not because I owed her, but because obedience would give *me* peace.

And it did.

My mother no longer remembers that she doesn't like me. You read that right. She doesn't remember.

In the last several months, she has been gentle. Kind. Grateful. She thanks me. Tells me she trusts me. Relies on me without resentment.

Some might call that vindication.

I call it peace—for her, and for me.

I do not desire a maternal relationship with her. I grieved that loss in 2012. That grief is complete. But I am grateful that my home is no longer a battlefield. That tension no longer lives in my body. That when she leaves this world, she will do so with dignity.

And I will do so with peace. Because what I realized is that peace isn't forgetting the past hurt it's learning to live healed within it.

I showed up.

I gave grace.

I honored her humanity—even when she could not honor mine.

And that is more than enough.

CHAPTER FOURTEEN: INHERITANCE INTERRUPTED

Lindsay,

I didn't raise you to be grateful for survival.

I raised you to expect freedom.

I had known tears in my life, but they had always been tied to survival whether shed through pain, sorrow, or fear. It wasn't until I became your mom that I learned tears could come from joy. You are my joy, Pumpkin.

There are moments in motherhood that change the trajectory of everything that follows. You don't recognize them as such when they happen. You only feel the shift later when you realize your decisions started orbiting a new center.

One of those moments was the day I walked through the door without a baby in my arms.

You were two. Too young to understand adoption, permanence, or choice. But you were old enough to know something had changed. One day, I was pregnant. The next day, I wasn't. And you felt that absence before I could find language for it.

You loved *The Little Mermaid*. It was your favorite bedtime story, your favorite movie, your most cherished book. When I walked through the door that day, you didn't cry the way adults expect children to cry. You didn't ask questions you couldn't yet form. You went straight to that book and ripped it to shreds.

Page by page. Deliberate. Final.

That moment gutted me in a way I've never fully recovered from. It seared itself into my soul. It was clear to me then that children grieve with their bodies and their actions when they don't yet have the words to speak loss aloud. And standing there, holding what was left of that book, I understood something else too.

I could not protect you from pain entirely.

But I could protect you from being alone in it.

That day became a vow I never spoke out loud but honored in every way I knew how. I would not disappear from your life. I would not dismiss your feelings. And I would never treat your heartbreak as something inconvenient or unworthy of care.

That vow shaped every decision that followed.

Even in those early years, there was something else I noticed.

In nearly every photo of you, there was a light.

It wasn't subtle. It wasn't accidental. A glow would appear near you or around you, sometimes soft, sometimes unmistakable. At first, I brushed it off as lighting or coincidence. But it kept happening. Repeatedly.

One day, your grandmother and I sat together and went through photo after photo. We stopped talking. The evidence was undeniable.

To me, that light meant something sacred. It meant that even when I was exhausted, scared, unsure, and carrying more than I thought I could, God was watching over you. His angels were present in ways I could not be.

As a single parent, that knowledge gave me comfort I can't fully put into words. In my darkest moments and seasons of great challenge, I knew you were held by something greater than me.

Never lose sight of this, Lindsay. You are God's child. All that you are does not come from me alone. It comes from Him, through me.

A few years later, on your fifth birthday, you handmade your invitations. They were uneven and joyful and perfect in the way only a child's confidence can be. I mailed eight of them, assuming two or three parents would decline. I was wrong. Every single one accepted. It turns out a New Year's Eve birthday reads like free childcare to adults.

You opened your gifts carefully, one by one. And then you reached one you didn't want. Your face shifted. Disappointment flickered. Dismissal followed. I felt it rise in me immediately, sharp, and protective.

But I didn't correct you publicly. I didn't embarrass you. I took you into your bedroom and closed the door.

I told you that someone had thought enough about you that they got in their car, drove to a store, walked the aisles, chose something just for you, stood in line, paid for it, drove home, wrapped it, spent their gas money to bring that gift to you. That was the gift. Their money. Their time. Their consideration.

That lesson stayed with you. I see it now in how you receive everything. Not just presents, but effort. Love. Presence. People still comment on your gratitude, your thoughtfulness, your ability to honor intention even when the outcome isn't perfect. That matters to me.

Because what I learned early, and hoped to pass on, was this: dignity does not require humiliation. Correction does not require shame. Strength does not require cruelty.

When you were nearly six, we were living in Phoenix. I was working full-time at Maricopa Health System and attending school full-time, trying to build a future with limited support. You were in daycare during the day. My uncle helped at night while I was in class. My mother had made it clear she was unavailable.

One afternoon, standing in that daycare, I noticed something I couldn't ignore.

You were the only chocolate drop in the room.

And I didn't like it.

I knew what it meant to be the "only." I knew how early isolation could teach a child to shrink, to assimilate, to accept being misnamed or misunderstood. I did not want that for you. I did not want you to learn to tolerate invisibility.

When I received a job offer in Los Angeles, we moved. Shortly after, I met Joyce, a colleague who became the big sister I never knew I needed. She told me about an all-Black private school her son attended. I enrolled you immediately.

It wasn't convenient. It wasn't cheap. Every dollar mattered. All my income went toward rent because safety was non-negotiable, and private school tuition and extended care came with a cost I felt every month. But liberation rarely arrives without sacrifice.

What you gained was priceless.

You learned who you were before the world tried to define you. You were surrounded by Black brilliance, Black care, and Black affirmation. You were bold. Confident. Unapologetic. You belonged without explanation.

From age seven to nine, I used to drive us through the wealthiest neighborhoods in Los Angeles. I parked my car, which clearly signaled we didn't "belong," and we walked anyway. I wanted you to see proximity without intimidation. To understand that space does not belong to one kind of person.

At home, we played a game. I would say, "You're thirty-two. Where do you live? What do you do? And where's Mommy?"

Your answers were almost always New York or Los Angeles. Entertainment. And me, nearby. Next door. One floor down.

I wanted you to soar. Truly. But knowing you felt anchored to me filled my heart in ways I still struggle to explain. Letting you go while wanting you close has always lived like a pendulum inside me. I learned to hold both.

As you grew older, I became even more intentional about something else.

Connection.

Today, families feel scattered in ways that go far beyond geography.

Distance is emotional now. Generational. Children grow up without knowing their elders, without hearing the stories that explain who they are and where they come from. I didn't want that for you.

Every summer, I sent you back to Clovis. You spent weeks with your great-grandparents, surrounded by cousins, great-aunts, great-uncles, and family history that couldn't be found in books. Sometimes you stayed with your grandmother in Phoenix. Sometimes with your grandfather in Amarillo. But Clovis was the anchor.

You were the first of your generation, and it showed. You learned how to listen to elders. How to sit still long enough to hear stories. How to belong to something larger than yourself.

You became the glue.

You are connected to your elders in a way that is rare now. You know the history. You know the names. You know the stories. You hold relationships across generations with ease and love.

You still tell me that those summers were your favorite childhood memories. And when I look at who you've become, I understand why.

That grounding mattered. It still does.

Legacy is not just what we leave behind. It's who we keep close.

Then there's the day at the park.

You were about nine. I was coaching an all-girls team. You ran over to a tree and stood beneath it. When I asked what you were doing, you said you needed to get out of the sun so you wouldn't get too dark.

Everything in me went still.

This was not anger.

This was fear.

I knew how quickly shame could take root if unchallenged. I knew the inheritance you were at risk of receiving. I could not allow you to reject what was naturally and beautifully yours.

I intervened.

I asked Mark, a friend I trusted, to casually tell you how beautiful your skin was. When he did, you beamed. Your shoulders squared. Your whole posture shifted.

That moment mattered.

There is another part of you I want to name here, because it matters deeply to me. Your fierceness. The way you defend and uplift the Black community with your whole chest, without apology, without shrinking. I watch you move through the world with a clarity and courage that both fills me with pride and, if I'm honest, terrifies me in equal measure.

I remember the first time you told me you were going to protest. My heart lodged itself somewhere in my throat. I had seen the footage. Police firing rubber bullets into crowds. Chaos erupting where people were simply demanding to be seen and valued. Every instinct in me wanted to pull you back, to shield you, to keep you safe. But I also knew that the very thing that scared me was the same thing that made me proud. You weren't marching for spectacle. You were marching because injustice offends your spirit. Because silence has never felt like an option to you.

You carry that same conviction everywhere. In the way you speak up online, knowing your words will be read, challenged, and sometimes misunderstood. In the way you choose how to wear your hair and dress your body, honoring your Blackness as expression rather than concession. In the way you amplify Black artists, educators, organizers, and advocates—not as a trend, but as a commitment. You don't just consume culture; you protect it. You don't just benefit from community; you pour back into it.

Watching you do this has been one of the great honors of my life. You move with a freedom I fought hard to give you, and a confidence I once had to borrow until I learned it was mine. You remind me that loving our people is not just about pride, it's about action, voice, and choice. I couldn't be prouder of the woman you are, or the way you stand firmly in who you are, even when the world pushes back. You are brave in ways I once had to learn. And seeing that bravery live so fully in you tells me the work mattered, and it didn't just happen by accident.

One day, without fanfare, I realized we were no longer living in preparation mode. We were simply, living.

Our trip in 2025 felt like a victory lap. Not the loud kind, but the kind you take after years of endurance. It was the moment when we finally took it all in and realized how far we've come. You have been my constant, my steady presence through a life that demanded resilience at every turn. There is no language big enough to hold the gratitude and love I feel for you.

So, I celebrated the only way I knew how. I planned a two-week adventure for just the two of us in Amsterdam and Italy. Your first time leaving the country. Our first trip wasn't shaped by basketball tournaments, family obligations, or survival logistics. This one was about joy. About curiosity. About us. I spared no expense, not out of extravagance, but intention. I wanted you to feel how deeply you are cherished.

It was unforgettable. We had so many beautiful moments full of laughter, wonder, long walks, and moments that felt suspended in time. A trip we will talk about for years. One that marked not just where we went, but who we had become. And it won't be the last. Just the first of many chapters written across new maps, together.

This is how the torch passes—not through perfection, but through presence.

I didn't do this life thing perfectly. Sometimes, I went left when I should have gone right. I made decisions I later revisited. But whenever I could course-correct, I did. And when I couldn't, I learned.

The work continues.

But the ground is different.

And that difference is you.

I love you immensely.

CHAPTER FIFTEEN: THE LOVE THAT NEVER LEFT

A letter to my second daughter, the one who lives beyond these pages.

I have started and stopped this letter more times than I can count.

Not because I lack words, but because I understand the weight they carry. How much tenderness. How much history. How much love. And how much complexity.

And I don't want to make this pretty.

I want to make it true.

I won't write your name here—not because I'm ashamed of you, and not because you are a secret. It's because I respect your privacy and your life. You deserve to be held with care, even on these pages.

But I need you to know this: you have never been missing from my story.

You are my second daughter. The daughter I placed. And you have been with me every day since the moment I knew you existed.

Even when I couldn't hold you the way I wanted to.

Even when I couldn't raise you the way I imagined.

Even when life moved forward, and the world expected me to "get over it" and keep going.

I did keep going. But I never went on without you.

When you found me—on LinkedIn, of all places, I was not prepared for what it would do to me. I remember reading your message and suddenly feeling like the air had left the room. I cried so hard I couldn't even make sense of the words at first. I was overwhelmed in a way I had never experienced before. I called David, trying to explain what had just happened, but I couldn't get the sentence out. He couldn't understand what I was saying, only that something extraordinary had just occurred. I couldn't believe that you had found me.

I've shared with you that when I placed you with your parents, there was a song that stayed with me then and has never left me. Most people hear "I Will Always Love You" by Whitney Houston as a romantic love song. I never did. When I listen to it, I hear us. I hear the hope I carried for you. That life would treat you kindly. That you would have space to dream. That joy would find you in unexpected ways. And more than anything, that love would always surround you.

And so, I carried you in ways no one else could see. You lived in my quiet moments. You lived in the choices I made. You lived in the way I worked, the way I fought, the way I built. You lived in the way I tried to become stable enough, strong enough, and successful enough to make sure at least one part of my story didn't end in loss.

Placing you for adoption was the hardest thing I have ever done.

And I need you to hear this clearly, without confusion: it was never because you weren't wanted.

It was because I loved you.

I loved you in the only way I knew how at the time. With fear and faith. With grief and conviction. With the kind of love that breaks a mother open and still says, "Let her have a chance."

I know that sentence might land heavy. I know it might raise questions that don't have clean answers. I'm not writing this letter to force anything. I'm not writing it to pressure you into closeness. I'm not writing it to rush your healing or mine.

I also need you to know that I don't require anything from you.

Not forgiveness.

Not comfort.

Not a relationship that moves faster than your spirit can handle.

Not constant communication.

Not certainty.

I don't want to be the kind of person in your life who makes love feel like an obligation.

If you need space, I will respect it. If you need silence, I will honor it. If you need time, I will not rush you. I will not punish you for protecting your heart.

But I do want to say something I don't want to leave unsaid.

Meeting you in person in November (2025) was one of the most sacred moments of my life.

Seeing you—seeing your face, your mannerisms, the way you move through the world—did something to me that I can't put into perfect language. It felt like God let me touch a miracle I had been praying over for years.

Looking into your eyes was overwhelming.

Something in me recognized you immediately.

You looked like me. And yet you were entirely your own. Whole. Real. Beautiful. A living story.

I remember thinking, *There you are.*

I didn't realize how much my heart had been holding its breath until that moment.

And I'm grateful beyond words that Lindsay was there too.

That the three of us could exist in the same space.

Not as a performance.

Not as a picture-perfect ending.

But as truth.

As family.

As something God allowed.

I know misunderstandings have happened. I know some things touched tender places—especially around your birth father. I want to acknowledge that without trying to defend myself or rewrite your experience.

The truth is: I haven't always known what you needed from me.

There were times in the past when you did not want information, and I tried to respect that. And when the desire shifted, I didn't handle every part of it perfectly. I see that now. I wish I had asked more questions instead of making assumptions. I wish I had slowed down. I wish I had created more room for you to lead.

But even in that, I want you to know something.

My love for you has never been fragile.

It has never depended on agreement.

It has never required proximity.

It has never needed you to perform gratitude.

It has never demanded that you make me feel better about anything.

It has simply been love.

And it still is.

You don't owe me access to your life to be worthy of my love.

You don't owe me closeness to be my daughter.

You don't owe me a certain kind of relationship for your existence to matter to me.

You matter because you are you.

And if the future holds reconnection, I will be grateful.

If it holds distance, I will still be grateful.

Because having the opportunity to meet you, to see you, to hug you, and hold that moment in my hands was a gift I will never take lightly.

I also want you to know this: you shaped my life.

There were days I kept going because of you.

There were seasons I worked harder because of you.

There were times I refused to give up because of you.

You were with me in every suit I put on and every battle I fought to build a stable life. You were with me in every prayer I whispered when I didn't have the strength for anything else. You were with me in the quiet moments when the world couldn't see what I was carrying.

Even when we had no contact.

Even when we were strangers on paper.

Even when I had no right to reach for you.

I still reached for you in my spirit.

Always.

So, this is what I want to leave you with, as simply as I can say it:

I love you.

I have always loved you.

I will always love you.

I am proud of you because of who you are, not what you do.

And no matter what happens from here, I will always be grateful that God allowed me to see you with my own eyes. To see your smile. To hug you.

If you ever come back to this letter in a moment of doubt, I hope it answers one question clearly:

You were never abandoned in my heart.

Not for one day.

Not for one breath.

Not for one lifetime.

With all the love in me,

Mom

CHAPTER SIXTEEN: THE LEADER I BECAME

For a long time, I equated leadership with control.

Not because I wanted to dominate anyone, but because control felt like safety. Control meant nothing could fall apart. Control meant my competence stayed unquestioned. Control meant I never had to ask for help, slow down, or admit I was exhausted.

Control was my survival strategy.

But somewhere along the way, I started to understand something that changed the way I led forever:

You can be excellent and still be exhausted.

You can be respected and still be depleted.

You can be powerful and still be performing.

And the truth is, I had spent too many years mistaking performance for power.

I wasn't just leading teams. I was leading outcomes, leading crises, leading integration efforts, leading meetings across time zones, leading people through uncertainty, and leading through change.

And on top of all that, I was leading the perception of me.

As a Black woman, composure is never neutral. It is watched. Measured. Interpreted. It is like living under surveillance where nobody announces the cameras, but you still feel them. You learn to keep your voice steady, your face calm, your delivery polished. You learn to make competence look effortless, even when it costs you everything.

So yes, I became excellent.

But excellence, I learned, does not equal access.

It does not equal protection.

It does not equal equity.

And it definitely does not equal peace.

The shift in my leadership didn't happen in one clean moment. It happened in pieces. Quiet, deliberate decisions. Small moments where I realized I was being invited to repeat old patterns. Moments where I could feel the old version of me stepping forward to carry what was never mine to carry.

Then I started choosing differently.

Not because I became softer.

Because I became clearer.

The Underperformer

I loved my one-on-ones with my team.

No matter how jammed my calendar got, no matter how chaotic the week felt, those 1:1s were sacred to me. That was our time. Our check-in. Our space to solve problems, clear obstacles, build a strategy, and strengthen trust.

They grounded me.

That week, my calendar was stacked like dominoes. Back-to-backs. Quick pivots. Meetings where everyone needed something. I remember feeling stretched thin, but still grateful. I had built a strong team. High performers. Leaders. People who carried their weight and then some.

All except one.

He was new-ish. A genuinely nice guy. Polite. Pleasant. The kind of person you want to root for.

And I did root for him.

We had already had conversations. Clear ones. Supportive ones. I laid out expectations. I gave him structure. I gave him time. For a while, it seemed like he improved. Two months of better responsiveness. Two months of stronger engagement.

Then the pattern returned.

He started rescheduling meetings at the last minute. Leaving calls early "out of nowhere." Showing up late. Being vague when clarity was required. Saying yes, but not delivering.

At first, I tried to make sense of it.

Maybe he was overwhelmed.

Maybe he needed more coaching.

Maybe the ramp-up was harder than I realized.

But that week, in our one-on-one, I finally saw it clearly.

Not in what he said—but in how he showed up.

He was physically there, but he wasn't really there. His energy felt distant, like he was already halfway out the door. Like his mind had disengaged long before his calendar did.

And I remember sitting there, listening to him speak, feeling something shift in me. Not anger. Not frustration.

Clarity.

Because I wasn't just noticing his performance anymore. I was feeling the weight of it.

I was having to lead calls I shouldn't have been leading. I was executing tasks that were his to own.

A major global implementation failed to land because he didn't take the ownership necessary to execute. And I had to jump in and get it across the line.

People noticed.

Not in a gossipy way.

In a business way.

Concerns started coming to me. Questions. Subtle hints from stakeholders that his reliability was becoming a problem. And I could feel what was coming next if I didn't act.

My team had worked too hard to build a reputation as a hub of excellence.
My team had earned trust through execution.

I had earned credibility through consistency.

I could not let one person's bare minimum ride on the backs of everyone else's excellence.

That was the moment I realized something important:

This wasn't a capability issue I could coach.

This was misalignment, and it was mine to confront.

Then the excuses started.

Doctor appointments.

Family situations.

Emergencies.

At first, I offered empathy. Life happens, I know that.

But eventually, the excuses became noise.

Then one day, he repeated an excuse he'd already used.

He told me something that could not possibly be true. It wasn't ambiguous. It wasn't "maybe." It wasn't a misunderstanding.

It was a lie.

Small, maybe.

But unmistakable.

And when I caught it, I felt the final click.

Because once someone starts lying to cover unreliability, the problem is no longer performance.

It's trust.

I sat with that for a moment after our meeting ended. My reflection faintly visible in the black rectangle of my laptop. And I remember staring at myself, not fully seeing myself.

Not because I didn't recognize my face, but because I didn't recognize the life behind it.

The leader.

The mother.

The fixer.

The family crisis captain.

The one who takes the lead when there's a death.

The one who handles what other people can't handle.

And in that quiet moment, I realized something else, too.

I had spent my entire life being the person who carries.

But leadership is not carrying people who refuse to walk.

So, I made the decision.

I didn't drag it out.

I didn't extend it again.

I didn't rewrite expectations a fourth time.

I named the reality plainly.

I told him the truth: the role required ownership, not attendance. The business needed someone who would execute what they were hired and paid to perform. This wasn't about his character. This was about fit.

And I exited him with dignity.

That was the difference between the old me and the new me.

Old me would have absorbed the work and made excuses. Old me would have protected the peace by carrying the burden silently.
Old me would have rationalized it away.

New me understood that protecting the culture was part of my job.

And I wasn't willing to let excellence be punished by tolerance.

The Promotion Fight

There is another kind of leadership moment that doesn't show up in performance reviews.

It doesn't get celebrated.

It doesn't make headlines.

It doesn't even look like leadership to most people.

It looks like paperwork.

Emails.
Justifications.
Budget conversations.

Meetings behind closed doors.

But I've learned that some of the most important leadership moments happen right there.

In the rooms where decisions are made about who gets to rise. I had a high performer on my team.

Exceptional.

Stellar reviews.

A top performer in the company for three years in a row. Not one complaint. Not about quality, timeliness, attitude, or execution.

He was beyond reproach.

And I knew he deserved a promotion and a pay increase.

I also knew what was coming.

Because I had lived it.

There is always an excuse: budget, timing, headcount, fiscal year.

And too often, Black and Brown excellence is expected to be grateful for visibility instead of being compensated for value.

But I was in leadership now.

And that meant I had a decision to make.

I could accept what had been done to me.

Or I could interrupt it.

I did what I always do when I'm serious about something.

I came with receipts.

Performance metrics.

Outcome summaries.

Leader praise.

Peer feedback.

A full record of contribution.

I made it undeniable.

And still, my manager resisted.

He told me we didn't have the budget.

Then he said something that made my stomach turn.

"We don't have a budget for this. Is there any way we can defer his compensation, or do you think he'll be expecting it now?"

I remember staring at him, feeling that sickening discomfort settle in my body.

Because there it was again.

The familiar dynamic.

A Black woman in a leadership seat having to appeal to a white man to do right by a Brown employee who had earned his due.

I wanted to ask him a hundred questions.

Since when do we defer pay for someone who earned it? Since when is budget convenience a reason to delay someone's livelihood?
Since when do we invent new rules only when the employee doesn't fit the preferred mold?

Instead, I said what needed to be said.

"I don't recall the company ever doing this to anyone else. Especially when I've been seeing all kinds of people being promoted lately."

I kept my voice calm.

Not because I was calm.

Because I was practiced.

I was not going to let my composure be used against me. I was not going to be framed as emotional or aggressive simply because I refused to comply with injustice disguised as process.

I left that conversation, and I knew exactly what was happening.

He was trying to make it inconvenient enough that I would drop it.

That is how inequity often works. It doesn't always show up as "no."

Sometimes it shows up as delay.

Sometimes it shows up as "next cycle."

Sometimes it shows up as "defer it."

Sometimes it shows up as exhaustion, hoping you will choose ease over advocacy.

But I didn't.

I stood ten toes down.

I fought. I justified. I escalated. I played the game because I understood the game. And when I couldn't find the money, I moved it.

I shifted budget from another area. It created scrutiny. It created tension. It created a few "no's" elsewhere.

But I would do it again.

Because he deserved it.

And because I knew something my manager either didn't understand or didn't care about.

When you deny someone what they earned, you don't just hurt them.

You teach everyone watching that excellence is optional. That loyalty is foolish. That contribution will be exploited.

And I refused to lead like that.

When the promotion and pay increase finally went through, I didn't celebrate.

I exhaled.

I waited until everything was finalized before I told him. I did not trust the system enough to speak too soon. I didn't want him walking around with hope that could be stolen at the last minute.

When I called him, he was happy. Grateful. Energized.

It was one of the best conversations you can have as a leader. The kind that reminds you why advocacy matters.

And I never told him how hard I fought.

I didn't want to burden him with the challenges behind the curtain. I didn't want to give him a reason to carry anger in his body.

All he needed to know was this:

His work mattered.

His excellence was seen.

And someone stood up for him.

I wasn't proud because I "won."

I was proud because when my moment came to do what had not been done for me, I did it.

The Whole-Self Shift

That's the thing about leadership growth.

It's not always visible.

Sometimes it looks like a quiet boundary.

Sometimes it looks like a hard decision made with dignity. Sometimes it looks like refusing to rescue someone at the expense of everyone else.

Sometimes it looks like advocating when it would be easier to comply.

Success used to mean being the one who could handle everything. Being the one who could carry anything.

Being the one who could stay composed no matter what.

Now, success means alignment.

It means I lead with empathy, but I do not abandon standards. I lead with grace, but I do not tolerate exploitation.

I lead with authenticity, but I do not perform for approval.

Power is not dominance.

It is influence through humanity.

It is protection.

It is stewardship.

Power is realizing you didn't just earn a lane. You earned the ability to build an on-ramp for someone who's still stuck on the shoulder.

And if I'm honest, that's what I want my legacy to be.

Not that I was exceptional.

But that I made it easier for someone else to be.

Because I no longer lead to prove.

I lead to build.

For a long time, I thought leadership meant being the fastest car on the freeway. The one that cruised freely. The one that did not stall. The one that did not need directions. I thought my job was to stay in motion at all costs. Merge. Accelerate. Outpace. Endure.

But over time, I learned something the freeway does not teach you. The best leaders are not the ones flying past everyone else. They are the ones who make it safer for other people to merge. They are the ones who slow down long enough to create space. The ones who do not weaponize power but use it like a signal light. Clear. Honest. Predictable.

That is what leadership became for me. Not about being the most impressive. About being the steadiest. Not safe as in comfortable. Safe as in clear. Safe as in consistent. Safe as in fair. Safe as in human.

That's the evolution.

That's Suits and Pajamas.

The grit to execute.

The grace to see people fully.

The wisdom to know when to hold, when to release, and when to fight.

And the courage to do it without needing permission.

CHAPTER SEVENTEEN: MY VOICE, OUT LOUD

I used to think reinvention was something people did when they didn't have responsibilities.

When life got quiet enough to daydream. When bills were paid. When the kids were grown. When you had the luxury of being uncertain for a while.

That wasn't my story.

My life never offered me long stretches of quiet. It offered me motion. It offered me pressure. It offered me problems that didn't care what season I was in. And for a long time, I wore that like proof of strength.

I was the woman people depended on.

At work, I was the one you called when something was urgent and messy. When a team was stuck. When the plan fell apart. When the stakes were high and someone needed to make a decision fast and stand behind it.

In my family, I was the same. When there was a death, I took the lead. When there was a crisis, I was the coordinator. When someone needed help, I was the person people expected to show up without being asked.

I never stopped to ask if it was mine to carry. I just carried it.

Because I had always done it.

But somewhere along the way, I started realizing something that made me uncomfortable.

The version of me that could carry everyone else was starting to disappear from herself.

I wasn't falling apart. I wasn't spiraling. I wasn't "breaking down" in the dramatic way people expect when they hear a story about change.

It was quieter than that.

I was functioning, but not flourishing.

I was effective, but not free.

I could still perform competently, like it was muscle memory, but I couldn't always feel myself inside my own life. I can't name the exact moment it shifted. I only know there came a day when my reflection felt like a stranger.

Not because she looked different.

Because she looked tired in a way sleep doesn't touch.

I had been so busy achieving, providing, leading, protecting, managing, and producing that I had stopped asking myself what any of it was for.

I didn't pause long enough to sit with myself. I didn't sit with myself long enough to understand myself.

What mattered to me.

What I wanted.

What I needed.

Who I was becoming.

And once you realize you've been living on autopilot, you can't unsee it. That awareness becomes a turning point, whether you're ready or not.

I didn't know it then, but that moment was the beginning of reinvention.

Not the kind you announce on social media.

The kind that happens in the soul.

Because reinvention, for me, wasn't about becoming someone new.

It was about returning to the version of myself I had buried under survival.

That's what people misunderstand. Reinvention isn't always a dramatic pivot. Sometimes it's an internal surrender. A decision to stop living in fragments. A decision to stop shrinking the truth just to keep other people comfortable.

For years, I had been mentoring people one-on-one.

Quiet conversations.

Phone calls.

Text threads that stretched late into the night.

Lunch meetings where I poured out wisdom, I hadn't even realized I was carrying.

Men and women alike would find me at work, pull me aside, and ask me questions they didn't feel safe asking out loud. Black and Brown people and women, especially. Women who were talented, ambitious, exhausted, and trying to make sense of systems that rewarded them only when they overperformed.

I didn't advertise it. I didn't label it. I didn't even call it mentoring most of the time.

It was just who I was.

If I had a map and someone else was lost, I couldn't keep it to myself.

But after a while, I started noticing something else.

That kind of mentoring wasn't sustainable.

Not because the people didn't deserve it. They did.

Not because I didn't love making a difference. I did.

But because the need was bigger than what one woman could hold through private conversations.

It wasn't just one person who needed clarity.

It was dozens.

Then hundreds.

And the more I poured out one-on-one, the more I realized I was trying to solve a systemic problem with personal bandwidth. I was trying to hold up other people while still holding up my own life.

And I could do it.

I had always been able to do it.

But managing isn't the same as sustaining.

But the question became: should I?

Because I was starting to understand that being needed isn't the same thing as being called.

And I was being called to something bigger.

That was the moment I stopped thinking of my voice as something I should manage and started seeing it as something I needed to release.

Not because I had all the answers.

Not because I wanted to be a guru.

Not because I thought I was an expert in all things.

I'm not.

But I *am* an expert in my experiences.

And I've lived enough life to know this: experience is not just something you survive. Experience is a credential. Experience is a classroom. Experience is proof that God can sustain you when life applies pressure meant to break you.

Suits & Pajamas was born from that truth.

Not as a marketing concept.

As a mirror.

Suits represent the part of me the world already knows. The executive. The operator. The woman who can walk into chaos and organize it. The woman who can lead global teams and deliver results. The woman who can stay composed under scrutiny, doubt, and deliberate underestimation.

Pajamas represent the part of me people don't always get to see. The woman who has carried grief. The woman who has fought for peace. The woman who has prayed when exhaustion felt louder than faith. The woman who has had to parent, provide, and protect while still healing herself.

For a long time, those two versions of me lived separately.

I would put on my Suit and become what the world required.

Then I would go home, put on my Pajamas, and finally exhale.

But healing required more than toggling between personas.

Healing required integration.

That's what this chapter is about.

Not success.

Not visibility.

Not reinvention for reinvention's sake.

This chapter is about wholeness.

Podcasting was one of the first ways I practiced that wholeness out loud.

The first time I recorded my voice, I was painfully aware of myself. I listened to my tone, my cadence, my pauses. I questioned everything. Was I too much? Was I not enough? Was I saying it right? Was I being too honest? Would someone misunderstand me? Would someone weaponize my truth?

Growth doesn't erase old instincts.

They show up when you're about to do something brave.

I almost talked myself out of it. I almost waited until I felt "ready," which for someone like me is code for "perfect."

But I didn't want perfect.

I wanted real.

So, I pressed record anyway.

And something unexpected happened.

People didn't connect to my resume.

They connected to my humanity.

When I shared pieces of my story, people started responding with their own. Not surface-level comments. Not polite encouragement.

Truth.

I started receiving messages from people who had never told anyone what they were carrying. People who were outwardly successful but privately exhausted. People who were doing all the right things but still feeling empty. People who were tired of being strong.

I realized my voice wasn't just a tool for leadership meetings.

My voice was a bridge.

And I wasn't meant to walk across it alone.

Public speaking deepened that.

There is a particular kind of vulnerability in standing in front of a room and choosing to tell the truth. Not the polished version. Not the version that makes people comfortable. The version that costs you something to say.

But I kept doing it because I kept seeing what it did for other people.

When you tell the truth, you give other people permission to stop hiding.

And that's the part I didn't fully anticipate.

I wasn't just sharing my story.

I was creating space.

Space for women who had been shrinking.

Space for leaders who were tired of performing without authenticity.

Space for Black and Brown professionals who had been carrying the invisible weight of code-switching, hypervigilance, and being "under surveillance" simply for existing in certain rooms.

I started to understand something I wish someone had told me earlier.

Leadership isn't about being the loudest.

It's about being the clearest.

It's about being consistent.

It's about being fair.

It's about being human.

It's about using whatever lane you've been given to widen the road behind you.

And that shift changed my definition of success.

Success used to mean control.

Success used to mean being untouchable.

Success used to mean staying ahead of the collapse by never slowing down.

Now, success means alignment.

It means I don't abandon myself to be accepted.

It means my values don't disappear when pressure shows up.

It means I lead with both grace and grit, because that is what my life demanded of me, and I refuse to pretend otherwise.

And most importantly, it means I'm not here to be seen as an expert in everything.

I'm here to be a witness.

To what God can do with a life that should have broken.

I'm not saying that like someone who has never been tempted to quit. I'm saying it as a woman who knows what it means to be tired in the bones. The kind of tired that sleep can't reach. The kind of tired that makes you wonder if you're still living, or just performing survival.

There were years I carried so much that I couldn't even tell what mine was anymore. Other people's emergencies became my calendar. Other people's needs became my schedule. Other people's expectations became my identity. I got used to being the one who handled things, fixed things, and solved things. I became so dependable that I forgot how to be human in public without explaining myself.

That's why this season matters.

Because this isn't me stepping into a spotlight for the sake of visibility. This is me using my voice because alignment demands it.

When I started podcasting, speaking, and writing, I wasn't trying to prove that I had all the answers. I wasn't trying to build a platform on perfection. I wasn't trying to become anyone's guru. I'm not an expert in all things leadership. I'm not an expert in trauma. I'm not an expert in healing.

But I am an expert in my lived experience.

I'm an expert in what it feels like to grow up in chaos and become a high-achieving adult who can lead a room but can't rest. I'm an expert in what it costs to be the "strong one" in a family system that never asks who holds you. I'm an expert in what it means to be a Black woman in corporate America, where your composure is monitored like evidence, and your excellence is treated like a requirement instead of a gift.

I'm an expert in survival.

And I'm learning to become an expert in freedom.

That is what Suits & Pajamas has always been, even before I had language for it.

It's the suit: the part of me that can walk into a room and lead, execute, negotiate, and deliver. The part of me that can build systems, manage crises, and stand tall under pressure.

But it's also the pajamas: the part of me that doesn't want to spend the rest of my life pretending I don't have needs. The part of me that refuses to keep calling exhaustion "discipline." The part of me that believes softness is not weakness, and rest is not laziness. The part of me that knows that healing doesn't require me to become someone else. It requires me to become myself.

For a long time, I mentored people one-on-one.

I did it constantly. Quietly. Faithfully. I poured into women who were trying to survive workplaces that didn't see them. I poured into leaders who were carrying teams while privately drowning. I poured into people who needed language for what they were experiencing because the workplace loves to call systemic harm "miscommunication."

I would take the calls. Read the drafts. Review the resumes. Rehearse the presentations. Coach through the tears. Help them strategize through politics they never asked to play.

I loved it. I still do.

But again, it wasn't sustainable.

Because I was giving out pieces of myself the way I used to: fully, quickly, instinctively, as if being needed was proof I was doing something right. I had to face a hard truth. I could not build impact with the same blueprint I used for survival. I could not keep pouring from a place that didn't refill.

I had to learn that my calling does not require my depletion.

And that's when something shifted.

Podcasting, public speaking, and writing became a new kind of mentoring. A wider kind. A more sustainable kind. Instead of trying to reach one person at a time, I could reach thousands. Instead of repeating the same truths in private conversations, I could speak to them publicly and let people take what they needed without me having to hold every piece.

I didn't stop caring. I started scaling care.

That is reinvention.

Not reinvention as image, but reinvention as obedience.

Because I know what it means to be on the other side of someone's courage. I know what it means to hear a story and suddenly have words for your own life. I know what it means to listen to someone say, "You're not crazy. You're not weak. You're not imagining it," and feel something unlock inside you.

That's what I want to offer.

Not perfection.

Permission.

Permission to rest without guilt.

Permission to tell the truth.

Permission to stop being loyal to systems that harm you.

Permission to build a life that fits you, instead of shrinking yourself to fit it.

In the beginning, I thought sharing my story was about courage. I thought it was about finally saying the things I had survived in silence. And yes, it took courage. But over time, I realized something else was happening. It wasn't just courage.

It was surrender in its purest form.

Because surrender is what happens when you stop trying to control the narrative and start letting God use it. Surrender is what happens when you stop polishing your pain into something palatable and instead let it be true. Surrender is what happens when you stop asking, "How will this make me look?" and start asking, "Who will this set free?"

I used to believe my story was something to outgrow.

Now I know it's something to steward.

There is a difference.

I am not here to be admired.

I'm here to be useful.

I'm here to be a witness.

To what God can do with a woman who had every reason to harden but chose softness anyway.

To what God can do with a woman who could have become bitter but chose clarity instead.

To what God can do with a woman who once believed she had to be exceptional to be safe and is now learning that she is safe because God is faithful.

The strangest part of all of this is that the more I tell the truth, the lighter I feel. I used to think truth-telling would expose me. That it would make me vulnerable in a way that could be used against me.

Instead, it made me free.

Because freedom is not pretending you were never hurt. Freedom is refusing to let hurt keep writing your future. Freedom is choosing to live whole, even when brokenness is what you know best. Freedom is waking up every day and deciding that you are no longer available for the version of yourself that only knows how to survive.

And I know this now in a way I didn't know before.

Success is not the goal.

Peace is.

Freedom is.

Authenticity is.

There was a time when I needed my life to look impressive so I could believe it was safe. Now I want my life to feel honest so I can finally live it.

That's the difference.

That's the evolution.

And that's what I'm carrying forward.

Not as a brand.

As a calling.

Because the scars that used to embarrass me have become bridges. The very places I once tried to hide are the places God keeps using to reach someone else. The wounds I once thought disqualified me are now the proof that healing is possible.

And I'm not finished.

I'm no longer running.

I don't measure my worth by survival anymore.

I measure it by freedom.

Not freedom as a finish line.

Freedom as a daily choice.

And that is where this memoir ends.

Not with a perfect bow.

Not with a dramatic conclusion.

But with a woman who finally knows she is allowed to live in freedom.

CHAPTER EIGHTEEN: CHOOSING FREEDOM

I used to believe freedom was something you earned.

That if I did enough, achieved enough, proved enough, survived enough, there would come a day when I could finally exhale. A day when my shoulders would unclench. A day when I could stop looking over my own life like a supervisor, checking for what might fall apart next.

I thought freedom was the reward.

But now I know better.

Freedom is not a finish line.

Freedom is a decision.

And women like me are experts at delaying it.

I postponed it for my family. For my daughter. For my job. For my reputation. For my own sense of duty. I postponed it because I had been trained to believe that my value lived in what I could carry, what I could endure, what I could make happen when no one else would.

I was praised for being strong, and I mistook that praise for love.

I was celebrated for being reliable, and I mistook that reliability for safety.

And I kept going.

Even when my body begged me to slow down.

Even when my heart begged me to feel.

Even when my spirit begged me to stop performing and start living.

For years, survival was my language. It was how I introduced myself to the world. It was how I earned belonging. It was how I stayed protected. Survival made me sharp. It made me capable. It made me successful.

It also made me tired in places that sleep could not touch.

The truth is, I didn't become who I am by accident.

I became her by necessity.

The child who learned to disappear became the woman who learned to lead.

The girl who learned to read moods became the executive who could read a room before anyone else noticed the temperature shift.

The teenager who learned to perform became the adult who could deliver excellence in environments that never intended to make space for her.

And for a long time, I wore that excellence like armor.

It protected me.

It also trapped me.

Because armor does not just block harm.

Armor blocks touch.

Armor blocks softness.

Armor blocks rest.

Armor blocks the kind of joy that requires surrender.

I didn't always know I was living inside a suit.

But I knew I couldn't take it off.

Not really.

Not all the way.

Not without feeling exposed.

Not without feeling like I was risking everything I had worked so hard to build.

Shaping Change

Somewhere along the way, my life began to change shape.

Not because the world became kinder.

Not because systems suddenly became fair.

Not because the freeway finally opened a lane built for me.

My life changed because I started telling the truth.

The truth about my childhood.

The truth about what it cost me to become "the strong one."

The truth about what it did to me to keep functioning while quietly falling apart.

The truth about my mother, and the grief that didn't come from losing her body, but from losing the hope of what she could have been.

The truth about my father, and the wound of his distance that shaped my expectations long before I had words for it.

The truth about my daughter, and the way motherhood became both my redemption and my revolution.

The truth about love.

The truth about God.

The truth about myself.

And once I started telling the truth, I could no longer pretend that survival was enough.

Healing Takes Time

Healing did not arrive in a dramatic moment.

It arrived in fragments.

In counseling sessions, I finally stopped trying to sound composed and started saying what was real.

On quiet mornings, I realized I didn't know what I liked, only what I could do.

In moments where my body reacted before my mind could explain it.

The first time I said "no" and didn't apologize for it.

The first time I rested without justifying it.

The first time I stopped chasing achievement as proof that I deserved peace.

It took years to unravel the lie that I had to earn rest.

Years to stop confusing exhaustion with purpose.

Years to stop equating struggle with virtue.

And slowly, something softened in me.

Not my ambition.

Not my excellence.

Not my standards.

What softened was my fear.

The fear that if I stopped pushing, I would disappear.

The fear that if I wasn't exceptional, I would be forgotten.

The fear that if I wasn't needed, I wouldn't be loved.

That fear had driven so much of my life.

It had also driven me away from myself.

A Legacy Worth Passing

Now, when I look back, I don't only see pain.

I see patterns.

I see how generational trauma can pass down like an inheritance no one asked for.

I see how women learn to survive by becoming smaller, sharper, quieter, and tougher.

I see how children learn to adapt by becoming useful.

I see how love gets distorted when people are raised without tenderness.

And I see the miracle in this:

I interrupted it.

Not perfectly.

Not without mistakes.

Not without grief.

But with intention.

With prayer.

With courage.

With the kind of love that chooses something different even when it has never seen an example.

When I placed my daughter for adoption, it devastated me.

It also woke me up.

It forced me to confront the direction my life was headed, and it demanded that I choose something else.

I didn't know then that this choice would ripple forward.

I only knew that I could not keep repeating what had been modeled for me.

I could not keep looking for love in places that would cost me my dignity.

I could not keep chasing acceptance at the expense of my peace.

And when Lindsay came into my life fully, I made a vow.

Not the kind you say out loud.

The kind you carry.

My daughter would not inherit my silence.

She would not inherit my shrinking.

She would not inherit my shame.

She would not inherit my fear of being too much.

She would inherit my truth.

And she did.

She is bold.

She is brilliant.

She is grounded.

She is deeply connected to her roots.

She knows who she is.

And she loves her Blackness without apology.

That is not accidental.

That is legacy.

Legacy used to mean accomplishments to me.

Degrees.

Titles.

Promotions.

The kind of success people could point to and say, "See? She made it."

Now, legacy means something else.

Legacy is what remains when no one is watching.

Legacy is what my daughter carries in her nervous system.

Legacy is what she believes she deserves.

Legacy is what she tolerates and what she refuses.

Legacy is the way she moves through the world with self-respect.

Legacy is the way she knows she can take up space without earning permission.

Legacy is the way she knows love should not require suffering.

Legacy is the way she knows she can be soft and still be strong.

Legacy is the way she knows she can be successful and still be free.

I did not just raise a daughter.

I raised a lineage forward.

I am an expert in my experience.

And my experience has become a lantern.

Not because I am special.

But because I finally stopped pretending.

This is where I am now.

I still work hard.

I still lead.

I still build.

But I no longer push the way I used to push.

I no longer chase achievement like it is oxygen.

I no longer need to prove that I deserve to exist in the room.

I no longer measure my worth by how much I can carry.

Now I measure my life by something else.

Peace.

Freedom.

Authenticity.

Alignment.

And the quiet joy of being present in my own life.

Living In Grace

If you are reading this and you see yourself in any part of my story, I want you to know something.

You are not crazy for being tired.

You are not weak for needing rest.

You are not ungrateful for wanting more than survival.

You are not selfish for choosing peace.

You are not broken for carrying what you carried.

You are human.

And you deserve to be free.

Not one day.

Not when everything is finished.

Not when everyone else is taken care of.

Now.

Because freedom is not an arrival.

It is a daily choice.

And today, I choose it.

I choose softness without shame.

I choose boundaries without guilt.

I choose truth without apology.

I choose joy without permission.

I choose a life that belongs to me.

Not the version of me that was built for survival.

The version of me that was built for love.

For purpose.

For peace.

For legacy.

For freedom.

And if my story becomes anything in the hands of the reader, I hope it becomes this:

Proof that the cycle can end.

Proof that healing can ripple forward.

Proof that your scars can become bridges.

Proof that you can build a life that does not require you to disappear.

I am no longer living to outrun my past.

I am living to honor what I survived.

And to make sure what tried to break me becomes the on-ramp I leave behind.

EPILOGUE

These days, my life is quieter.

Not empty. Not small. Not perfect. Just quieter in the way a soul becomes quiet when it finally stops fighting for air.

Some mornings, I sit with my coffee and listen to the house wake up. The hum of the AC. The sound of David moving around in the kitchen. The faint sounds of birds remind me of the promise of the day ahead. My mother, still here, still living in the upstairs apartment, still moving through her days with memories that come and go like the weather.

Sometimes she wakes up sweet. Sometimes she wakes scared. Sometimes she wakes up confused or agitated, even when she doesn't mean to.

And yet, the strangest miracle of all is this: my body no longer braces the way it used to.

For most of my life, I lived with a kind of internal readiness. A vigilance that never powered down. Even in peace, I was preparing for war. Even in joy, I was scanning for what might take it away.

That is what survival does to you. It teaches you to hold your breath even when no one is chasing you.

But now, I exhale.

Not because everything is solved, but because I finally understand something I never knew as a little girl: peace is not a reward. It is a posture. A decision. A way of living that says, *I will not abandon myself to prove I can endure.*

I used to think freedom would feel like arriving.

Now I know freedom is not an arrival. It is a daily choice.

It is choosing not to pick up burdens that were never yours.

It is refusing to explain your worth to people committed to misunderstanding you.

It is saying no without guilt. Resting without earning it. Letting quiet be quiet.

It is remembering that endurance is not the same as strength, and performance is not the same as purpose.

There is a part of me that will always remember the old road.

The long stretches of my life where I was building and driving at the same time. Raising my daughter. Climbing in corporate America. Leading teams. Managing crises. Mentoring others. Carrying family emergencies. Carrying generational pain like it was simply part of the job description of being a Black woman.

For a long time, I thought the goal was to master the system. To become so capable, so indispensable, so excellent that nothing could touch me.

But that was never the goal.

That was just the coping mechanism.

The real goal was always deeper: to become whole.

To hold power without performing for it. To lead without losing myself. To love without bracing for impact. To live without constantly rehearsing the worst-case scenario as if it were wisdom.

That is what I am now.

Not flawless. Not finished.

But present.

I look at Lindsay, and I see what all of this was for.

She isn't perfect either. But she is free in ways I wasn't allowed to be at her age. She knows herself. She trusts herself. She speaks up. She takes up space. She loves her Blackness like it is a birthright, not a burden.

And that didn't happen by accident.

It was taught. Protected. Reinforced. Defended.

I remember the moments people might overlook.

The way I watched her in classrooms for signs she was shrinking.

The way I moved her into environments where she could see herself reflected as beautiful, intelligent, and worthy.

The way I took her into neighborhoods where we weren't expected and made sure she understood: nothing is above you.

The way I corrected her privately, so dignity stayed intact.

The way I refused to let shame settle into her bones—because I knew how quickly it could.

There is a photo of Lindsay when she was little, and if you look closely, you can see it. A light. A strange, unmistakable glow that appeared again and again across different pictures, different moments, different places.

My mother noticed it too. We sat together once, going through photos like detectives, trying to explain it away.

But I never could.

Some people might call it reflection, camera flare, or coincidence.

I called it covering.

To me, it was evidence that even when I felt alone, I wasn't. That even in my darkest seasons, God had her. God had us.

I've had moments in my life where I didn't know how I was going to make it.

But I did.

Not because I was so strong.

Because God was faithful.

And because I never stopped choosing to get up.

That's what I want you to understand about my story: I am not here to be admired.

I am here to be a witness.

To what God can do with a life that should have broken.

For years, I mentored people one-on-one. I loved it. I still do. I love seeing people awaken. I love watching them step into their voice. I love helping them name what they've been carrying and why.

But I learned something important.

That kind of mentorship is sacred, but it isn't scalable. It isn't sustainable. And it isn't the only way to serve.

My voice had to grow beyond private conversations. Beyond phone calls. Beyond the "real quick" questions that were never quick.

So I began speaking.

Podcasting.

Writing.

Not because I am an expert in all things, but because I am an expert in my experience—and testimony is its own kind of leadership.

Some people lead with titles.

Some lead with authority.

I lead with truth.

That is what *Suits & Pajamas* has always been about.

It's not about having it all together. It's about showing up whole.

It's knowing how to wear your armor when necessary and knowing how to take it off when it's time to breathe.

It's bridging grace and grit.

It's building your own on-ramp when the freeway wasn't built for you.

And if I've learned anything, it's this: legacy is not what you accomplish.

Legacy is what you pass down.

Not just money. Not just credentials. Not just property.

But self-worth.

Boundaries.

Nervous system peace.

Faith that holds you when you can't hold yourself.

The kind of freedom that lets the next generation live, not just survive.

I still remember the little girl I used to be—the one who learned early that adults were unpredictable. The one who learned to disappear. The one who learned that excellence could be a shield.

I lived too long under surveillance, too long under the pressure to be perfect, too long afraid that one wrong move would confirm every stereotype.

But I do not live there anymore.

I belong to myself now.

And I belong to God.

So, if you close this book and remember nothing else, I want you to remember this:

You do not have to keep proving you deserve peace.

You do not have to keep earning rest.

You do not have to keep sacrificing yourself on the altar of being "strong."

You are allowed to build a life that feels like freedom.

And if you come from what I come from, if you've survived what I've survived, then you already know this:

The freeway was never designed for us.

But we have always been builders.

So build.

Build the life.

Build the peace.

Build the legacy.

Build the road your children will not have to bleed on.

Because what tried to break you does not get the final word.

It gets repurposed.

It becomes the on-ramp, the map, and the merge lane for everyone who comes after you.

And that, to me, is what freedom looks like.

ACKNOWLEDGEMENTS

This book was not written alone.

Even when I was the only one in the room, even when I carried things no one else could see, even when my voice felt like it had to stay inside my chest for safety, I was never truly alone. God was with me. He placed people in my life who became shelter, scaffolding, and strength.

There are chapters in this memoir that were hard to write, not because the memories were unclear, but because the truth was. Some will judge me. Some of these pages cost me tears. Some cost me pride. Some cost me the version of myself that still wanted to be misunderstood, because being misunderstood was easier than being fully seen.

But I wrote it anyway.

Because I believe stories are bridges. And I believe God never wastes pain.

And so, I thank you God.

Thank You, Lord, for keeping me. For covering me when I didn't know I needed covering. For correcting me when I thought I was right. For holding me steady when my life looked strong on the outside but felt fractured on the inside.

Thank You for not letting me become hard. Thank You for not letting me become bitter. Thank You for not letting me confuse survival with purpose.

Thank You for giving me a voice and then giving me the courage to use it.

To my husband, David.

You changed my life in ways I didn't know were possible.

You did not enter my story trying to fix me, tame me, or take credit for my healing. You simply showed up. You stayed. You loved me with consistency, not performance. You gave me a safe place to soften. You gave me partnership when I had only ever known responsibility.

Thank you for all the years of meeting me at the car after long days. Thank you for the breakfasts and lunches you packed because you knew I would forget. Thank you for the baths you drew, the calm you carried, the selfless caring for my mom, and the steadiness you offered without asking me to earn it.

You taught me that love can be peaceful. That trust can be built slowly. That protection can be gentle and yet strong. That marriage can be "Us vs. the problem," even when the problem is old wounds trying to speak louder than the present.

I love you.

To my daughter, Lindsay.

You are my greatest assignment and my greatest joy.

You have been the most beautiful evidence that generational cycles can change. You are proof that what tried to break me did not win. You are proof that softness can be strength. That boundaries can be holy. That Blackness must be worn like a crown and not a burden.

There were times I didn't get it right. There were times I was too tired, too stressed, or too focused on making sure our life didn't collapse. There were moments I went left when I should have gone right. But hear me clearly: every decision I made was rooted in love. Fierce love. Protective love. The kind of love that was determined to give you what I did not receive.

Thank you for growing into the woman you are. You have made me proud in every era of your life.

You are the legacy.

To my other daughter, L.

There is no way to write of you in this book without my heart warming.

You have been with me, even when you were not physically with me. You have been with me in my prayers, in my quiet moments, in the pauses between achievements, and in the grief, I learned to carry without collapsing.

I want you to know something I hope you never forget you were never abandoned in my spirit. Not for one day. Not for one season. Not for one breath.

That decision was not the absence of love. It was the most painful expression of love I have ever known. And while I will always carry the weight of that moment, I also carry the truth of you.

Thank you for allowing space for communication. Thank you for allowing connection to exist in whatever way it can. Thank you for being part of my journey, even from a distance, even through complexity.

I love you. Always.

To my brother, Wil.

You were my first protector. My greatest, bestest friend. Our wonder twin powers are activated for life.

You were the first person who made me feel safe in a world that often didn't. You were my witness and my partner in survival. We learned how to read rooms early. We learned how to guard ourselves early. We learned how to carry weight that wasn't ours to carry.

And even with all of that, we found a way to love each other through it. I will always have your back. I will always love you more than words can express. And nothing and no one will ever change that.

Thank you for being my brother, my friend, and my forever bond - my true touchstone in life. Thank you for staying connected through every version of life. Thank you for being the one person who always understood the unspoken.

To my stepchildren, and to my grandchildren.

To my stepchildren: blended families don't always come with easy lanes or clear rules, but I appreciate you both making space for me in a way I don't take for granted. Thank you for allowing me to love you, support you, and show up for you. I'm not going anywhere.

And to my grandchildren. You are joy made visible. You are my heart's favorite song on repeat.

You are laughter in the house and light in every room you enter. You are the sound of God's goodness echoing through generations. You are proof that family can expand, love can multiply, and connection can be chosen on purpose.

Thank you for letting me love you freely, fully, and without limits.

Every time I look at you, I'm reminded that freedom is real because you are living in it.

I love you with every ounce of my being.

Forever your Lolli, your Grandma (and whatever beautiful name the future decides to give me), I love you all so very much.

To my extended family.

To my amazing nephews, nieces, aunts, uncles, cousins, and elders: thank you for the village. Thank you for the prayers. Thank you for the summers in Clovis that grounded my daughter in family history and deep roots. Thank you for the stories, the laughter, the meals, and a love that transcends struggle and misunderstandings. We are love personified.

To my parents,

There is so much I could say, but what matters most is this: I forgive you.

I forgive you for what you did.

I forgive you for what you didn't do.

I forgive you for what you didn't know how to give.

I understand now that you were carrying pain long before I ever arrived, and that some of what I experienced was the overflow of what you never had the chance to heal.

I release every grievance. I release every unanswered question. I release the hope that the past could be rewritten.

I pray that your remaining years are filled with love, peace, dignity, and rest.

And I pray that God meets you gently in the place's life was not.

I honor the fact that you gave me life. And I choose to let the rest go.

To my chosen family.

Thank you for being the kind of people who loved me through seasons I couldn't explain. Thank you for checking on me. Thank you for laughing with me. Thank you for not requiring perfection from me. Thank you for reminding me that strength doesn't mean isolation.

Thank you for being safe place.

To every mentor, sponsor, and leader who opened doors.

Thank you to those who saw my excellence and did not punish me for it. Thank you to those who advocated for me when it wasn't convenient and when I wasn't in the room. Thank you to those who valued my voice, not just my output.

And to those who made it harder: you also played a role. You sharpened me. You forced clarity. You taught me what kind of leader I would never become.

To the readers.

If you are holding this book, I want you to know something:

I wrote this for the part of you that has been carrying too much for too long.

I wrote this for the woman who looks successful but feels exhausted. For the woman who has been surviving so long that she forgot what freedom feels like. For the woman who keeps showing up for everyone else but hasn't been able to show up fully for herself.

May these pages remind you that you are not alone.

May they remind you that your story is not over.

May they remind you that healing is possible.

And may they remind you that peace is not something you earn.

It is something you choose.

ABOUT THE AUTHOR
T'Juana Albert

T'Juana Albert is a corporate leader, author, speaker and founder of Suits & Pajamas, a platform built on the idea that real leadership happens at the intersection of who we are at work and who we are at home. With more than two decades of experience navigating corporate America, she is known for leading with clarity, empathy, and conviction—bridging grace and grit in rooms where both are often in short supply.

Through her writing, speaking, and podcasting, T'Juana explores the intersections of identity, ambition, faith, and legacy, offering language for the quiet exhaustion many high-achieving women carry but rarely name. She lives in Florida with her husband, David, and remains deeply rooted in family, community, and the belief that freedom is something we choose to build on purpose.

Ways to Stay In Touch:
http://www.suitsandpajamas.com/
http://www.tjuanaalbert.com/